Contents

About the Authors 5

Introduction 6

Chapter 1   The Priesthood of Believers:
            an Autobiography 8

Chapter 2   The Priesthood of Believers
            and the Bible 25

Chapter 3   The Priesthood of Believers
            and Salvation 44

Chapter 4   The Priesthood of Believers
            and the Church 59

Chapter 5   The Priesthood of Believers
            and the Christian Life 78

Chapter 6   The Priesthood of Believers
            and Spiritual Gifts 95

Chapter 7   The Priesthood of Believers
            and the State 111

Chapter 8   Your Priesthood and Your World 126

Teaching Guide 143

The Church Study Course 158

About the Authors

A native Mississippian, Dr. Walter B. Shurden is Callaway Professor of Christianity and chairman of the Department of Christianity at Mercer University in Macon, Georgia. He has taught church history at McMaster Divinity College in Hamilton, Ontario, Canada; Carson-Newman College; and the Southern Baptist Theological Seminary in Louisville, Kentucky. He is a graduate of Mississippi College and New Orleans Baptist Theological Seminary and has pursued postdoctoral studies at the University of Tennessee and Princeton Theological Seminary.

Dr. Shurden has also served as president of the Southern Baptist Historical Society and as chairman of the Historical Commission of the Southern Baptist Convention. He has spoken widely at denominational gatherings and college campuses.

His wife, Dr. Kay Shurden, is a family therapist and educator and presently serves as associate professor in the Department of Family and Community Medicine at the Mercer Medical School in Macon, Georgia. The Shurdens have three grown children: Sherry, Paula, and Walt.

Dr. Shurden has written four books: *Not a Silent People: Controversies That Have Shaped Southern Baptists; Associationalism Among Baptists in America, 1707-1814; The Sunday School Board: Ninety Years of Service; The Life of Baptists in the Life of the World.*

The teaching guide for this book was written by Dr. Arthur H. Criscoe. Dr. Criscoe is the director of the Management Support Group, Church Training Department of the Sunday School Board of the Southern Baptist Convention. He is also the author of *The Doctrine of the Priesthood of Believers— Teaching Workbook.*

Introduction

Fred Craddock told in a sermon about returning to his small west Tennessee hometown each Christmas. Every year he would visit an old friend named Buck. Buck owned a cafe on the main street of the town, and he always gave Craddock a cup of coffee and a piece of chess pie.

One Christmas when Craddock went in to get his coffee and pie, Buck said, "Come on, let's go get a cup of coffee." "What's the matter?" asked Craddock. "Isn't this a restaurant?" "I don't know; sometimes I wonder," Buck fired back.

Later, sitting across from Craddock, Buck asked, "Did you see the curtain?" "Yes, Buck, I saw the curtain; I always see the curtain." The curtain was in Buck's cafe, separating the front half of the restaurant from the back half. White folk came in the front of the cafe from the main street, but black folk came in from an alley behind the cafe. The curtain was there to separate people.

Buck looked up and said, "Fred, the curtain has got to come down." "Good," Craddock responded. "Bring it down!" "That's easy enough for you to say," said Buck. "You come in here once a year and tell me how to run my business." "Then leave it up," Craddock countered. In personal agony, Buck said, "Fred, I take that curtain down, and I lose my customers; I leave that curtain up, and I lose my soul!"

The doctrine of the priesthood of believers is about curtains coming down. "Jesus cried again with a loud voice and yielded up his spirit. And behold, the curtain of the temple was torn in two, from top to bottom . . ." (Matt. 27:50-51). The curtain was one, but symbolized in the curtain and the Jewish Temple were many separations: people from God, laity from clergy, females from males, Gentiles from Jews, and secular from sacred.

The doctrine of the priesthood of believers cuts across most major theological themes of the Christian faith. This doctrine influences our theology (doctrine of God), Christology (doctrine of Christ), ecclesiology (doctrine of the church), and soteriology (doctrine of salvation). But it also speaks to issues of worship, baptism, the Christian life, stewardship, ministry, and biblical interpretation.

But the priesthood of believers addresses more than Christian doctrine. It speaks to how we live and act as God's people. It says that the individual cannot be denied, the church cannot be ignored, the world cannot be forsaken, the ministry cannot be restricted, and the state cannot be idolized. It has brought meaning and purpose to the lives of individual disciples, theological revolution and spiritual revival to the church, redemption and healing to society, and confrontation and conflict with kings and political rulers.

If you trace them through Christian history, its advocates make a long and impressive list. Included are George W. Truett, E. Y. Mullins, Isaac Backus, John Leland, Roger Williams, Thomas Helwys, John Smyth, Philipp Jakob Spener, Martin Luther, Paul of Tarsus, and Jesus of Nazareth. The doctrine is rooted in the Bible, has made periodic appearances in Christian history, is grounded in Christian theology, and has many practical implications for the life of faith.

I first discovered the doctrine of the priesthood of believers shortly after I became a Christian as a freshman in college and joined the Second Baptist Church of Greenville, Mississippi. M. E. Perry, my pastor, gave me a little book introducing me to the meaning of the Christian life and of membership in a local Baptist church. E. R. Pinson and Howard Spell, my Bible professors at Mississippi College, taught me more about the priesthood of believers. Later, W. Morgan Patterson and Claude L. Howe, Jr., professors at the New Orleans Baptist Theological Seminary, increased my appreciation of the doctrine and helped me place it in a broader perspective through courses in Christian and Baptist history.

I have watched Christians in a number of local Southern Baptist churches struggle to live out the priesthood of believers, but nowhere any better than at First Baptist Church, Ruston, Louisiana; Crescent Hill Baptist Church, Louisville, Kentucky; and First Baptist Church, Macon, Georgia. Like most other people, I can preach, lecture, and write about it better than I can live it. It is, however, a doctrine to be lived. I invite you to learn it if you never have, to relearn it if you have forgotten it, but above all, to live it.

Chapter 1
The Priesthood of Believers: an Autobiography

Allow me to introduce myself. I am the Doctrine of the Priesthood of Believers. But do not let the word *doctrine* frighten you. It merely means *teaching*. Above all, do not permit the word *doctrine* to turn you off. I certainly am not a cold or abstract or irrelevant theological idea.

To the contrary, I pulsate with life. In fact, I am operative every day of your life. You may reject me, avoid me, minimize me, abuse me, or use me, but you cannot completely ignore me. I am present when you choose who will be the Lord of your life, and there is nothing abstract about that.

And as for irrelevance, well, you should know that I am front and center in the Bible. Also, I was one of the major discoveries of Protestant reformers such as Martin Luther and John Calvin. Many claim, and with good reason, that I am the centerpiece of the Baptist faith. My place in biblical teaching, Christian theology, and Baptist heritage is secure and firm. So do not back up from the fact that I am a doctrine. I am the very opposite of cold, abstract, and irrelevant. I matter immensely.

I am a doctrine, but my proper name is Priesthood of Believers. *Believers!* That is clear enough, isn't it? My last name refers, of course, to Christians who are believers in the proposition that Jesus Christ of Nazareth is the final and ultimate revelation of the eternal God. *Believers!* That "the Word was with God, and the Word was God . . . and the Word became flesh and dwelt among us, full of grace and truth" (John 1:1,14). *Believers!* That "in Christ God was reconciling the world to himself" (2 Cor. 5:19). *Believers!* That Jesus is "'the way, and the truth, and the life'" (John 14:6).

Believers! That part of my name is doubtless clear enough to you. But what about my first name—Priesthood? Can you think of a word that sounds more unbaptistic than *priest* or *priesthood?* It is almost as foreign sounding to a Baptist audience as *pope* or *bishop,* isn't it?

The truth is I have helped make you Baptists what you are today. You should not, therefore, be surprised that Findley B. Edge opened the 1986 Baptist Doctrine Study book on *The Doctrine of the Laity* with this sentence: "The doctrine of the priesthood of all believers is a fundamental belief among Baptists."[1] He was right on target.

But what does my first name mean—Priesthood? Just for fun, I looked me up in Funk and Wagnall's two-volume *New Comprehensive International Dictionary of the English Language.* Here is what I got: "priest: one especially consecrated to the service of a divinity, and serving as mediator between the divinity and his worshipers in sacrifice, worship, prayer, teaching, etc." Three words down I found: "priesthood: the priestly office or character." Just as I expected! Wooden, verbose, and inexact. Dictionaries are not to be trusted completely for biblical and theological language.

Let me clean up the definition and give it to you straight and simple. Priest: someone who relates to and acts for God. Priesthood: to be priestly, to relate to and act for God. Believers: disciples of Jesus Christ.

That's the definition. Here is the meaning: "All believers are priests." Every Christian—and I do mean *every Christian*—is "to relate to and act for God." Let me spell it out in more detail by telling you who I am and where I came from.

Who Am I?

Who or what am I? I am many things! I am biblical! I am Christian. I am Baptist. I am believers' rights. I am your right of direct and immediate access to God through Jesus Christ. In the words of one of the greatest Christians of you all, "There is one God, and there is one mediator between God and men, the man Christ Jesus" (1 Tim. 2:5). And because of the mediatorial work of Christ Jesus, each of you can "with confidence draw near to the throne of grace" so that you "may receive mercy and find grace to help in time of need" (Heb. 4:16).

I am your right to choose Christ for yourself. Nobody else can choose Him for you. Nobody else can stop you from choosing. You must choose Him all by yourself.

Joshua placed it before the people years ago: " 'Choose this day whom you will serve'" (Josh. 24:15). Jesus reduced the entire matter to two words: " 'Follow me'" (Mark 1:17). The choice is yours. I urge people to take responsibility for their lives.

But I have noticed that some of you folk will do almost anything to avoid the pain of accepting the responsibility for your lives. You will quote other people, talk like other people, let other people talk for you and even choose for you. Sooner or later, however, after you have finished with all the "some say . . . others say" routine, Jesus will back you up against the wall, and you will have to answer the question " 'Who do you say that I am?' " (Matt. 16:15). I am not only your right to choose; I am also your responsibility to choose.

I am the very opposite of proxy religion. Stand-ins won't work. Spectator religion is out. Personal participation is all that counts.

I am the democratization of faith. When Jesus died, "the curtain of the temple was torn in two, from top to bottom" (Matt. 27:51). And that meant theological revolution! That meant the Jewish high priest who had exclusive rights to the holy of holies was out of work. The holy presence of God was now available to all believers. That ripped curtain, "torn in two, from top to bottom," signaled that all believers now have equal "access in one Spirit to the Father" (Eph. 2:18).

I am essentially a movement of the people of God. I refuse to knuckle under to an autocracy of professionals. I am the antithesis of the attitude expressed in the address of Pope Pius X in 1906 titled *Vehementer Nos:* " 'As for the masses, they have no other right than that of letting themselves be led, and of following their pastors as a docile flock.' " I am a proud protest against authoritarianism of any kind and all kinds.

I object to power and privilege being concentrated in the hands of an elite few. I demand responsible participation in church life as well as in salvation. Someone related to me the incident of a Southern Baptist pastor invited by a pulpit committee to meet with the deacons of the church for preliminary conversations. After the usual light chitchat, they got down to business. One of the deacons, a delightful wholesale grocer, looked at the candidate and said, "Sir, what one question do you want most to get answered from us?" Almost immediately, the prospective pastor shot back: "I want to know if you have a free and open pulpit. Do I have the freedom to say from this pulpit what I honestly think God wants me to say?" The deacon who asked the question responded. "Yes," he said slowly and deliberately, "we have a free pulpit." Then he added, "But we also have a free pew." I cheered! There a grocery man was, protecting me, standing up for me and all Baptists everywhere. I demand responsible participation. That is why a late Anglican bishop, Kenneth E. Kirk, referred to me as "the decisive formula of all non-episcopal Christendom."[2]

I am not *office* by virtue of ordination. I am *relationship* by virtue of God's grace and calling. I am not something you have. I am not even first of all something you do. I am something you are. It belongs to your very being as a child of God to *be* a priest. As 1 Peter 2:9 says, "You are . . . a royal priesthood."

The rest of that verse is equally important. It tells you something else about who I am: "You are . . . a royal priesthood." But then the writer adds "that you may declare the wonderful deeds of him who called you out of darkness into his marvelous light." I am *responsibility.*

Fulton Sheen, the late, well-known Roman Catholic archbishop, once proposed that since America had a statue of liberty on the east coast, the country should also establish a "statue of responsibility" on the west coast. As I have indicated in the previous paragraphs, I am certainly your symbol of freedom. While never minimizing the freedom part of my personality, I insist that I am also responsibility.

Your priesthood means that you are called and that you should "lead a life worthy of the calling" (Eph. 4:1).

Your priesthood means that you are gifted and that you are to use your gift "for the common good" (1 Cor. 12:7).

Your priesthood means that you are accountable for the way you use the good things God places in your hands (Matt. 25:14-30).

So you see, I am the freedom to "reach up in faith," but I am also the responsibility to "reach out in love." I am your privilege of access to God through Jesus Christ; I am your obligation of ministry in the world in the name of Christ. You are a priest *before* God, and you are priest *to* neighbor. I am a gift, and I am a demand.

McDonald's restaurants had an advertisement some time back in which they declared, "We do it all for you." Not so in the church! The clergy and the professional church staff are not there to "do it all for you." They could not if they wanted to, because there are not enough of them. Even if they wanted to, they *should* not. They would be arrogating to themselves what is your proper role as a priest.

That is why I am referred to in Christian history as the universal priesthood of believers. And that is why you Baptists have occasionally dubbed me the "priesthood of *all* believers." I am universal, not clerical. I am all believers, not a few. Paul said, "I appeal to you therefore, brethren, by the mercies of God, to present your bodies as a living sacrifice" (Rom. 12:1). To whom was Paul appealing with the pronoun *you*? Certainly not to the clergy of Rome! He was exhorting *all* the Roman Christians. *Every* Christian is to make a priestly sacrifice to God—the "living sacrifice" of one's entire being to God. I am the Priesthood of Believers, and the Believers part of my name is plural.

Where Did I Come From?

Like you, I have a history and a heritage. I came to expression in the early life of Israel as depicted in the Old Testament Scriptures. The New Testament reaffirmed me, as did the Protestant reformers and later your Baptist ancestors.

Origin in biblical teachings. If you are only nominally acquainted with the Old Testament, you surely know that the concept of priesthood is prominent throughout that book. The Hebrew word for *priest* is *kohen.* It is used over seven hundred times in the Old Testament. *Kohen,* a noun, is associated with the verb *kahen,* which probably means *to stand.* So a priest, a *kohen,* is one who stood before God as servant or minister.

The key passage as far as I, the Priesthood of Believers, am concerned is Exodus 19:4-6. The background of those verses is crucial. Moses, that cheerleader for justice, had led the children of Israel out of captivity in Egypt. Pharaoh's forces had been overcome, and some of the wilderness perils had been surmounted. The people of Israel now stood before the sacred mountain where God first appeared to Moses. Before they could strike their tents and be on their way to the Promised Land, their relationship to God needed to be sealed with an agreement. The Old Testament refers to this agreement as a covenant.

So there they were before the mountain, Moses, and Almighty God. It was a pivotal moment in Hebrew history. And here is what the Bible says in Exodus 19:3-6:

Moses went up to God, and the Lord called to him out of the mountain, saying, "Thus you shall say to the house of Jacob, and tell the people of Israel: You have seen what I did to the Egyptians, and how I bore you on eagles' wings and brought you to myself. Now therefore, if you will obey my voice and keep my covenant, you shall be my own possession among all peoples; for all the earth is mine, and you shall be to me a kingdom of priests and a holy nation."

That was the invitation of God to the people. It was an invitation to all Israelites to be priests, to relate to and act for God. What followed was the response of the people. It is recorded in Exodus 19:7-8:

So Moses came and called the elders of the people, and set before them all these words which the Lord had commanded him. And all the people answered together and said, "All that the Lord has spoken we will do." And Moses reported the words of the people to the Lord.

Israel had agreed to be a kingdom, and their king was to be Jehovah God. All the subjects of the king were to be priests. Other important developments concerning priests and priesthood in the Old Testament will be identified in the next chapter, but I am not concerned with those at the present. For the moment I want you to understand that I am rooted in the Old Testament and in the covenant that God made with *all* His people.

Birthed in the Old Testament, I came to fruition in the New Testament. The Greek word for *priest* is *hiereus*. It is used a number of times in the New Testament, especially in the Gospels and Acts, to describe the religious leadership of Judaism. On one occasion it is used to describe the actions of a "priest of Zeus" (Acts 14:13). None of these references, however, are significant for me.

14

Five New Testament passages, however, refer directly to me. These are found in the Books of 1 Peter and Revelation. They are: 1 Peter 2:5; 2:9; Revelation 1:5-6; 5:9-10; 20:6. Later you will need to look at those verses more carefully but underline this one fact for the present: *Israel's vocation and calling to be a kingdom of priests had become the vocation and calling of Christian believers.*

Note the way John opens his book to the seven churches of Asia:

Grace to you and peace from him who is and who was and who is to come, and from the seven spirits who are before his throne, and from Jesus Christ the faithful witness, the firstborn of the dead, and the ruler of kings on earth. To him who loves us and has freed us from our sins by his blood and made us a kingdom, priests to his God and Father, to him be glory and dominion for ever and ever (Rev. 1:4-6).

First-century Christians applied Exodus 19:6 to themselves. The priesthood of Israel became the priesthood of believers! So in 1 Peter 2:9 the persecuted and perplexed Christians were reminded of who they were: "You are a chosen race, a royal priesthood, a holy nation, God's own people." The similarity in that language and Exodus 19:6 is not even subtle, is it? It was not intended to be!

You should know two other things about me in the New Testament. First, I—the Priesthood of Believers—am inextricably related to the Priesthood of Christ. *Hiereus* is used in the New Testament to refer to Christ, but He is called the "great high priest" (Heb. 4:14) who "offered up himself" (Heb. 7:27). What He did has much to do with who I am and how I function in the Christian church. His sacrifice made freedom of access to God possible and love of neighbor mandatory.

A final thing about me in the New Testament. The title of priest is never used by New Testament writers to refer to a select and special group of Christians. It never means *clergy* or *ministers.* It has no reference to people who have yielded to "full-time Christian service." The priesthood belongs to *all* believers. The priesthood is *universal* throughout the church.

Development in Christian history. Following the first century, I began to have a rough time. In fact, from the second through the sixteenth centuries I played a minor role in the Christian church. Although not totally stamped out, I was so sufficiently shoved to the margin of the church's life that my influence was sadly neutralized. Those are days (and centuries) I would rather forget.

What happened? Three tragedies. Priesthood was clericalized! Grace was sacramentalized! Church was institutionalized!

Priesthood was clericalized! The clergy took me over "lock, stock, and barrel." The church began to stress the priesthood of *some* believers rather than the priesthood of *all* believers. Instead of having an inclusive priesthood, the church condoned the emergence of an exclusive priesthood. "Class-ism" invaded the body of Christ. That meant separation on the one hand and exaltation on the other. Whereas I was one in the New Testament, I got separated into two distinct classes of Christians, clergy and laity. And the separation between the two was clearly symbolized by the imposition of celibacy on the professional priests. And exaltation! The equality among believers in the New Testament gave way to hierarchy, the domination of the priests over the laity.

Grace was sacramentalized! The separation and exaltation of the clergy were made secure by the way that sinful humanity received the grace of God. Sacraments, such as baptism and the Lord's Supper, dispensed by the church through the clergy, became the accepted means of communicating grace and salvation. Sacramental faith replaced personal faith. Mediated access to God through the priests usurped direct access for the believers through Jesus Christ. In a sense, the temple curtain that had been torn asunder at the death of Christ was stitched together again. Believers were now led into the holy of holies by the professional priesthood, not by the Great High Priest.

Church was institutionalized! Church became a place to go rather than a people on the go, a building superintended by clergy rather than the body of Christ alive and active in the world through the laity. Those who were called in the New Testament to be participants in the ministry of Jesus Christ were transformed into spectators. *Lay* became a synonym for *amateur.*

These trends, so prevalent in medieval Catholicism, are obviously ruinous for the health and spiritual vitality of the church. And they are as devastating for Baptists in the twentieth century as for Roman Catholics in the twelfth century. When I get subordinated to the work of the clergy, the church is in need of reformation and renewal. Church is not church by virtue of its "ministers." Church is church by virtue of its Lord and *all* whom He calls.

Reformation came in the sixteenth century through the courageous witness of Martin Luther, John Calvin, Ulrich Zwingli, and other protesting leaders. Shocked by the actions of the medieval priesthood and disgusted by the definition of priesthood advocated by the church, they revolted. In the process they sought to restore me to my proper place in the Christian community.

Luther, the impulsive German who made so many contributions to the church, led the way. Personally, I owe him more than I can say. He brought me front and center in Christian doctrine. Scripturally, he found me in those New Testament passages to which I have already alluded: 1 Peter 2:5; 2:9; Revelation 1:5-6; 5:9-10; and 20:6. Additionally, he made much out of Jesus' words in John 6:45: "It is written in the prophets, 'And they shall all be taught by God.' Every one who has heard and learned from the Father comes to me."

Theologically, Luther rooted me in his famous doctrine of justification by faith. In his tedious and revolutionary study of Romans and Galatians in which he expounded that doctrine, he also discovered the clue to the unity and solidarity of all Christian believers. He loved Galatians 3:28, in which the apostle Paul says, "There is neither Jew nor Greek, there is neither slave nor free, there is neither male nor female; for you are all one in Christ Jesus." Reflecting on the meaning of that verse for his day, Luther wrote, "'There is neither priest nor layman, canon or vicar, rich or poor, Benedictine, Carthusian, Friar Minor, or Augustinian, for it is not a question of this or that status, degree, order.'"[3]

In 1520 Luther wrote three treatises that constituted the core of his protest against the church of his day. They were titled *To the Christian Nobility of the German Nation, The Babylonian Captivity of the Church,* and *The Freedom of a Christian.* All hard-hitting documents, the last catapulted me again into prominence. Said the fearless professor of Wittenberg:

> *Christ has made it possible for us, provided we believe in him, to be not only his brethren, co-heirs, and fellow-kings, but also his fellow-priests. Therefore we may boldly come into the presence of God in the spirit of faith [Heb. 10:19,22] and cry "Abba Father!" pray for one another, and do all things which we see done and foreshadowed in the outer and visible works of priests.*[4]

He added, "Injustice is done those words 'priest,' 'cleric,' 'spiritual,' 'ecclesiastic,' when they are transferred from all Christians to those few who are now by a mischievous usage called 'ecclesiastics.'"[5]

In 1544, near the end of his life, Luther was still lifting me up in his preaching. One scholar summarized Luther's emphasis of me with the following four points.

1. *Before God all Christians have the same standing, a priesthood in which we enter by baptism and through faith.*
2. *As a comrade and brother of Christ, each Christian is a priest and needs no mediator save Christ. He has access to the Word.*
3. *Each Christian is a priest and has an office of sacrifice, not the Mass, but the dedication of himself to the praise and obedience of God, and to bearing the cross.*
4. *Each Christian has a duty to hand on the gospel which he himself has received.*[6]

To repeat the obvious, I am grateful to Luther and other Reformation leaders for reaffirming me as an important Christian doctrine. They gave me a new lease on life. Sad to say, I remained throughout much of Protestantism more rhetoric than reality. That has always been one of the problems I've faced.

Prominence in Baptist life. As much as any other body of Christians, you Baptists have been my advocates. And I was no afterthought or Johnny-come-lately doctrine with you either. John Smyth of England, often called the first Baptist, wrote explicitly of me in 1608. In describing what he called "the Kingdom of the Saynts," Smyth said, "The visible Church by the Apostle is called a Kingly preisthood. 1. pet. 2. 9. and the Saynts are Kings & Preists vnto God Revel. 1. 6."[7]

Smyth spoke of the priesthood of the church (a phrase to which I am partial), and he described the work of the priesthood in general but biblical terms: "The saynts as Preists offer vp spirituall sacrifices acceptable to God by Iesus Christ. 1. pet. 2. 5."[8] He then gave an example, related to local church life, of the extent of this priesthood. Even if the church is without what he called an elder (pastor), it nevertheless has the "powre to Preach, Pray, Sing Psalmes, & so by consequent to administer the seales of the covenant: also to admonish, convince, excommunicate, absolve, & al other actions eyther of the Kingdom or preisthood." Even after the church has chosen and ordained its pastors, said Smyth, "the Church leeseth none of her former powre."[9] Don't forget that!

The father of you Baptists, while certainly not exhausting my meaning, launched your denomination on a lifelong romance with me. Writing almost three and one-half centuries later, Ernest A. Payne, one of the best-known names among English Baptists in the twentieth century, identified three ideas essential for an understanding of Baptists. These are: (1) the necessity for each person to make his or her own commitment to Christ; (2) the understanding of the church as a community of believers; and (3) the affirmation of the priesthood of all believers.[10] While Payne identified me by name in number 3, I am also vitally related to numbers 1 and 2, as well.

Having read a good bit of your literature, I have observed something about you Baptists. You have a difficult time agreeing on the precise language for describing your single most distinguishing denominational distinctive. But I have also noticed another fact. Whatever language you use, I am always very close to the center of your thought. Let me give you three examples of what I mean.

Example 1: John D. Freeman, standing before the first meeting of the Baptist World Alliance in 1905, preached a powerful sermon titled "The Place of Baptists in the Christian Church." "The Baptist denomination," he proclaimed in lyrical language, "is not an accident, nor an incident, nor an experiment; it is the normal development and permanent embodiment of a great Christian principle."[11] Guess what he said. Baptism by immersion? Wrong! The authority of Scripture? Wrong! Congregational church government? Wrong! Religious liberty? Wrong! However, he acknowledged all of these as thoroughly Baptist.

Freeman got wordy, as preachers sometimes do. Here is what he said is the "essential" Baptist principle: "*An acute and vivid consciousness of the sovereignty of Christ, accompanied by a steadfast determination to secure the complete and consistent recognition of His personal, direct and undelegated authority over the souls of men.*"[12] Read it again, slowly this time.

Later in the sermon Freeman summarized his cumbersome sentence into a more succinct expression—"the undelegated sovereignty of Christ." What did he mean by that phrase? You may never have heard it, but it was somewhat common to your ancestors. Freeman meant that Christ is sovereign in salvation. "To Christ, and to Christ alone, the individual must stand or fall," he said, and "there can be no proxy in the matter."[13]

But he also meant that because Christ is sovereign over the individual, neither the state nor anything else could or should be sovereign. He called that soul liberty, which he said issued into personal and civil liberty. "The undelegated sovereignty of Christ" is one of my theological foundations. You may want to think of it as one of my many synonyms.

Example 2: E.Y. Mullins, president and professor of theology at the Southern Baptist Theological Seminary from 1899 to 1928, was also president of the Southern Baptist Convention for 1923-24 and president of the Baptist World Alliance for 1923-1928. He was "Mr. Southern Baptist" in the first third of the twentieth century. Trusted widely, he was the primary author of The Baptist Faith and Message. Adopted in 1925, this was Southern Baptists' first confession of faith.

Maybe the most important and influential book Mullins wrote was titled *The Axioms of Religion.* Read it sometime! In that book Mullins asks: "What is the historical significance of Baptists? What great principle have they contributed to the religious thought and life of mankind?" His answer is "the competency of the soul in religion."[14] "To speak of the competency of the human soul sounds like the exact opposite of "the undelegated sovereignty of Christ," doesn't it? One stresses the human, the other the divine. Actually, they represent opposite ways of approaching the same truth.

Mullins was not speaking of human self-sufficiency. He never came close to suggesting that a Christian believer was independent of God, Christ, or the Bible. Human competency for Mullins was a competency under God. He was saying that each individual reaches God through Christ without any other mediator.

Moreover, Mullins meant that the individual believer has the right to read, interpret, and obey the Scriptures, the right of an equal voice in the church with other believers, the right of freedom of religious expression from state interference, and the responsibility to love his neighbor as himself. Does all that sound familiar in light of my description of who I am? Mullins said that I am a "corollary" and "derivative" of his identifying Baptist distinctive. Truth be told, I think it is the other way around. Else he was simply using another name for me and did not recognize it.

Other leading Southern Baptists of the twentieth century have echoed Mullins. George W. Truett served as pastor of the historic First Baptist Church of Dallas, Texas, for forty-seven years. Albert McClellan exalted him as one of the spiritual architects of the Southern Baptist Convention.[15] Truett hailed the competency of the soul as "the keystone truth of the Baptists." "Out of this cardinal, bed-rock principle," Truett said, "all our Baptist principles emerge."[16]

Over the past three decades of Southern Baptist life Herschel H. Hobbs has been probably your most prominent denominational statesman. Longtime pastor of the First Baptist Church, Oklahoma City, and president of the Southern Baptist Convention during some of the turbulent sixties, Hobbs was the primary author of Southern Baptists' second confessional statement. He also revised and updated Mullins's *The Axioms of Religion,* published in 1978 by Broadman Press. Taking the position of Mullins and Truett before him, Hobbs has repeatedly declared that "the competency of the soul" is the major Baptist distinctive.

Example 3: Norman W. Cox, executive secretary of the Historical Commission of the Southern Baptist Convention from 1951 to 1959, wrote a book in 1961 titled *We Southern Baptists.* He used one sentence to describe what is most distinctive in the Baptist concept of the Christian faith. *"It is,"* he said, *"redeemed personality ministering under the lordship of Jesus Christ, as revealed in the Scriptures."*[17]

Cox did not mention my name in his sentence. His explanation, however, made it clear he was talking about me. Here is his explanation:

> *Baptists have consistently recognized the immediate, direct authority of Jesus Christ as their Redeemer, Saviour, Lord, and Teacher. Because of these relationships Baptists have felt themselves to be called by Christ to obedience in life, faith, witness, and service.*[18]

Again, does that sound familiar? Two phrases in Cox's explanation capture the dual sides of me. They are "the immediate, direct authority of Jesus Christ" and "called by Christ to obedience." The first is access to God; the second is ministry to neighbor. In the first is communion; in the second is community. The first is the gift of priesthood; the second is its demand.

Now, after looking at Freeman, Mullins, and Cox, do you understand why I said you Baptists have a hard time agreeing on common language to describe your basic doctrinal distinctive? For Freeman it was "the undelegated sovereignty of Christ." For Mullins and Truett and Hobbs, "the competency of the soul." And for Cox, *"redeemed personality ministering under the lordship of Jesus Christ, as revealed in the Scriptures."*

Call it what you wish. But any way you describe it, you eventually get back to me. And for that, I thank you! I would remind you, however, that naming me is one thing. Doing me is another thing.

Well, that is who I am and where I've come from. In the rest of this book, the author will take a stab at describing what I mean for you. I hope he gets it right.

PERSONAL LEARNING ACTIVITY 1
List the most important points concerning the priesthood of believers that you would use to explain the doctrine to another person.

1. _____

   _____

2. _____

   _____

3. _____

   _____

4. _____

   _____

5. _____

   _____

Notes

1. Findley B. Edge, *The Doctrine of the Laity* (Nashville: Convention Press, 1985), 9.

2. Kenneth E. Kirk, *The Apostolic Ministry* (London: Hodder & Stoughton, 1946), 48.

3. E. Gordon Rupp, "The Age of the Reformation 1500-1648," *The Layman in Christian History,* ed. Stephen Charles Neill and Hans-Ruedi Weber (Philadelphia: The Westminster Press, 1963), 138.

4. Martin Luther, *Three Treatises* (Philadelphia: Fortress Press, 1960), 290-291. Used by permission.

5. Ibid., 291-292.

6. Rupp, 139.

7. *The Works of John Smyth,* (Cambridge: Cambridge University Press, 1915), 274.

8. Ibid., 275.

9. Ibid., 315.

10. Ernest A. Payne, *The Free Church Tradition in the Life of England* (London: SCM Press LTD, 1944), 174-176.

11. J. D. Freeman, "The Place of Baptists in the Christian Church," *The Life of Baptists in the Life of the World,* ed. Walter B. Shurden (Nashville: Broadman Press, 1985), 19.

12. Ibid.

13. Ibid.

14. E. Y. Mullins, *The Axioms of Religion* (Philadelphia: The Judson Press, 1908), 53.

15. Albert McClellan, *Meet Southern Baptists* (Nashville: Broadman Press, 1978), 38.

16. George W. Truett, "The Baptist Message and Mission for the World Today," in Shurden, 113.

17. Norman W. Cox, *We Southern Baptists* (Nashville: Convention Press, 1961), 5.

18. Ibid.

Chapter 2
The Priesthood of Believers and the Bible

In chapter 1 you read an overview of the doctrine of the priesthood of believers. It was by nature introductory, a way to get us into the general subject. The purpose of this chapter is more specific. Here we are going to examine in further detail what the Bible says about priesthood.

We shall look at three specific topics, all of which enhance a fuller understanding of the doctrine of the priesthood of believers. First, we shall survey the meaning of priesthood in the Old Testament. It is crucial to understand the development of the Jewish priesthood, if one is to interpret many of the books in the New Testament. More importantly, however, to understand early Christianity, you must see how it thoroughly changed from the priestly character of ancient Judaism. "The most conspicuous feature of the concept of the Christian priesthood in the New Testament is its radical transformation of the counterpart concept of the Israelite priesthood in the Old Testament."[1]

Second, the high priesthood of Christ, particularly developed in the Book of Hebrews, needs to be studied. The nature of Christ's priesthood helps to explain the early Christians' understanding of their own priesthood. Third, we will look explicitly at the five so-called priesthood passages in 1 Peter and Revelation.

The Jewish Priesthood
In his autobiography in chapter 1, Priesthood of Believers proudly told you that the Hebrew word for *priest* is mentioned seven hundred times in the Old Testament. He also said that the key passage, as far as he was concerned, was Exodus 19:4-6, in which God speaks through Moses to Israel at Sinai:

You have seen what I did to the Egyptians, and how I bore you on eagles' wings and brought you to myself. Now, therefore, if you will obey my voice and keep my covenant, you shall be my own possession among all peoples; for all the earth is mine, and you shall be to me a kingdom of priests and a holy nation.

Although he did not utilize it, Priesthood of Believers could have also used Isaiah 61:5-6 to underscore his contention that all Israelites were priests. Those verses say that aliens shall stand and feed your flocks, foreigners shall be your plowmen and vinedressers; but you shall be called the priests of the Lord; men shall speak of you as the ministers of our God. The argument that Israel was a corporate priesthood is sound and accurate. Certainly New Testament writers relied on these two passages (Ex. 19 and Isa. 61) to make their case for a universal priesthood.

One item, however, Priesthood of Believers failed to mention: most of the seven hundred references to *priest* in the Old Testament do not refer to the priesthood of *all* Israelites; they refer to the priesthood of *some* Israelites. Such numbers do not minimize the truth that Israel as a whole was to be a priestly people. But those numbers do require a further look at the meaning of priesthood in the Jewish community.

Under Moses a "professional," representative priesthood emerged in the life of Israel. The Jewish priesthood symbolized the covenant nature of Israel's life. It represented Israel's union with the Lord God.

After the ratification of the covenant (read Ex. 24:1-11) between God and Israel, which stated that Israel would be "a kingdom of priests and a holy nation" (Ex. 19:6), Moses spent "forty days and forty nights" on Mount Sinai. During that time God gave to Moses instructions that were to govern Israel's communal life and worship. Exodus 25:1 to 31:18 describes these detailed instructions, while Exodus 35:1 to 39:43 and Leviticus 8:1-36 explain how the instructions were implemented.

Included in these instructions was God's mandate for constructing the tabernacle and its furnishings and for the preparation and installation of the priesthood. Tabernacle! That was the "tent of meeting" where Israel would worship God. Priesthood! These were the people who mediated the divine-human meeting.

Meticulous care was given to both the dress (Ex. 28:1-43) and the ordination of the priests (Ex. 29:1-46). Both of these—the clothing and the consecration of the priesthood—are filled with rich symbolism about the nature of Israel's God and the purpose of the priesthood. We shall look at some of this symbolism in the following paragraphs. But for the moment underscore the fact that the idea of a special priestly group in Israel was no passing fancy.

One entire book of the Bible—Leviticus—is devoted to the role of the priesthood. So the concept of a select priesthood is embedded deep within Israel's history. We shall view the Jewish priesthood from only three angles: (1) the theological roots of the priesthood; (2) the function of the priesthood; and (3) the nature of the priesthood. These three are important because they form the background needed for understanding how early Christians reinterpreted the meaning of priesthood.

The theological roots of the priesthood. When I was a seminary student, Elton Trueblood, the popular Quaker theologian, delivered some lectures to our faculty and students. In one of his speeches he talked about the importance of conveying spiritual truth through symbolism. He illustrated with a personal experience. One day on a city bus he observed a woman unobtrusively making the sign of the cross as they passed in front of a Roman Catholic church. It dawned on him that Protestants have no symbolic counterpart to demonstrate reverence for the house of God, where so many people have found meaning and mystery, forgiveness and wholeness. Then half in jest, but with some seriousness as well, he suggested that maybe Protestants should reverently tip their hats as they travel past their churches!

The priesthood symbolized profound spiritual truth for Israel. First, priests represented *God's saving acts* on behalf of Israel. Through their leadership in worship, the priesthood literally represented God's intervention in history for Israel's salvation. God had lifted Israel out of Egypt on "eagles' wings" and had made this nobody people into a somebody nation. God had met Israel at Sinai and graciously entered into covenant with them. The law of Sinai was in reality the grace of God, unrequested help for the living of their lives. And they were never to forget it.

At the conclusion of the instructions for the ordination of the priests, God promised to meet His people at the tabernacle through priestly mediation: "I will consecrate the tent of meeting and the altar; Aaron also and his sons I will consecrate, to serve me as priests" (Ex. 29:44). After promising to "dwell among the people of Israel," God gave the intended result: "They shall know that I am the Lord their God, who brought them forth out of the land of Egypt that I might dwell among them" (Ex. 29:46). By their consecration to serve God, the priests were *living reminders* of what God had been for Israel—grace!

Second, priestly activity symbolized *God's loving presence* in the midst of Israel. For the Hebrews, God was no abstract argument. He was no philosophical question to be resolved. He was no far-fetched fancy conjured in a fevered mind. God not only acted for Israel; God also stayed with Israel!

The tabernacle said that! The word means *dwelling* or *dwelling place.* Synonyms for *tabernacle* said that, too. The tabernacle was "the tent of meeting," the "sanctuary," the "tabernacle of the Lord." Let them make me a sanctuary, that I may dwell in their midst" (Ex. 25:8), said the Lord.

The priests were the caretakers of the tabernacle. The rules for worship in Israel reflected the fact that priests did their work "before the Lord." Attention to details of priestly garments were significant, partially at least, because the priests were going "before the Lord" (see Ex. 28:12,29-30,35,38). Through their dress, their care for ritual purity, and their activity—intercession, mediation, and instruction—the priesthood reflected a fundamental theological concept of the Hebrew faith. Priests were *living witnesses* of what God continued to be for Israel—presence!

Third, the priesthood, above all else, symbolized *God's holiness.* As a covenant people, Israel was called to reflect the holy character of God. "You shall be to me a kingdom of priests and a holy nation" (Ex. 19:6), God had said. The overarching theme of the Book of Leviticus, in which the priesthood is so prominent, is that Israel must be a holy people because they serve and worship a holy God.

"I am the Lord your God; consecrate yourselves therefore, and be holy, for I am holy. . . . For I am the Lord who brought you up out of the land of Egypt, to be your God; you shall therefore be holy, for I am holy" (Lev. 11:44-45).

This dimension of holiness expressed itself in many ways in the life and worship of Israel, but nowhere more clearly than in the priests. Their dress reflected God's character and Israel's calling. Priestly vestments were to be "holy garments" (Ex. 28:2,4). Priests ministered in "the holy place before the Lord" (Ex. 28:35). Significantly, the initial step in priestly ordination involved the symbolic washing away of all things unclean (Ex. 29:4).

One of the important rituals in the ordination of the priests was the offering of the ram of ordination. (See Ex. 29:19-21.) In a highly symbolic gesture some of the ram's blood was placed "upon the tip of the right ear of Aaron and upon the tips of the right ears of his sons, and upon the thumbs of their right hands, and upon the great toes of their right feet" (Ex. 29:20). Applying the blood to the extremities represented the cleansing of the entire body. The priests, thereby, were made fit for the holy service of a holy God. Just as the priests were *living reminders* of God's saving acts and *living witnesses* to God's continuing presence, they were also *living examples* of God's holiness.

The functions of the priesthood. The Jewish priesthood served various functions at different eras in Israel's history. And to be sure, the priesthood maintained no monopoly on priestly functions during Israel's long tradition before Christ. To summarize, and all too briefly, we shall focus on two persistent purposes of the priesthood. These are intercession and interpretation. Priests were mediators who brought the people to God, and they were teachers who brought God to the people. This dual role is set forth most clearly in the blessing of Moses upon Levi. It is found in Deuteronomy 33:8-11. After lauding Levi, one of the original tribes of Israel set apart for the priesthood, for loyalty to the word and covenant of the Lord, Moses gave the charge in verse 10: "They shall teach Jacob thy ordinances, and Israel thy law; they shall put incense before thee, and whole burnt offering upon thy altar."

Priests were interpreters. They brought God to the people. The prophet Malachi, living probably in the fifth century before Christ, indicted the priests of his day because they failed to be good teachers of the covenant. Even in his criticism, however, Malachi knew what had been one of the major priestly functions: "The lips of a priest should guard knowledge, and men should seek instruction from his mouth, for he is the messenger of the Lord of hosts" (Mal. 2:7).

What kind of instruction did Israel seek from the mouths of priests? Almost every kind. Foremost, however, priests instructed the people on questions of right and wrong. Interpreting the law, they distinguished between "the holy and the common, and between the unclean and the clean" (Lev. 10:10). This included, among other things, what to eat, matters of hygiene, and medical diagnosis. (See Lev. 11—15.) Priests were custodians of culture and carriers of tradition. They taught God's ordinances and law.

Priests were also mediators. They brought the people, sins and all, to God. Both priestly dress and priestly acts indicated this function. One feature of the priestly garb consisted of two shoulder pieces. On each shoulder piece was fixed an onyx stone. And on each stone six of the names of the tribes of Israel were inscribed. When the priest went "before the Lord," therefore, he symbolically took the people with him (Ex. 28:5-14). But note what happened: one man entered the holy presence of God on behalf of all the people.

Nowhere is the mediatorial role of the Jewish priesthood more poignantly portrayed than on the annual Day of Atonement. Described in Leviticus 16, this was not the work of just any priest on any day. Only the high priest could enter the holy of holies on this special day once a year. Both architecture and personnel marked the separation of the high priest from the people and of God from the community at large. Access was limited. But the purpose was noble: to rid people of the heavy weight of guilt and to provide forgiveness for their sins. (See Lev. 16:33-34.)

The structure of the priesthood. As has been implied, generalizations about the Jewish priesthood are just that—generalizations. The specifics of origin, purpose, and nature are buried in a mass of historical detail that continues to keep our very best scholars busy. We need to note only two other generalizations. One is the hierarchical structure of the priesthood. The other is its hereditary nature.

Over a period of time the priesthood developed an elaborate bureaucracy. Gradations appeared within the priesthood itself. Sanctity was graded. The people at large were at the bottom of the scale. Next came the Levites, then the priests. At the top was the high priest. These three groups formed a spiritual elite, but some were obviously more elite than others. The foundations of these levels of holiness in Israel's history go back as far as Aaron. Jesus' marvelous parable of the good Samaritan included both a priest and a Levite, each of whom "passed by on the other side" of a stripped and beaten man (Luke 10:27-37).

Levites were minor clergy. As the name suggests, they were descendants of the tribe of Levi. They did not, however, come from the prestigious line of Aaron. Their work was circumscribed to secondary temple duties, but they had no part in the central acts of sacrifice. That was the exclusive duty of priests, people who could trace their genealogical roots back to Aaron. Two of the most famous senior adults in the New Testament, Zechariah and Elizabeth, were of this lineage (Luke 1:5). The hierarchy culminated in the high priest. He alone had the privilege of entering the holy of holies once a year to make atonement. With this intricate structure of clergy, it is little wonder that laymen are described in Leviticus as outsiders, especially if they were not of the priest's household (Lev. 22:10).

The priesthood was also hereditary. Ancestry and sex determined who would be priests. Birth, not worth, blood, not gift gave to one the priestly vocation. This restriction was doubtless partially due to the special knowledge required, easily passed on within a family. But this restriction also led to incompetency and the occupation of the priesthood by people uncommitted to their lofty role. These problems brought down the ire of the prophets more than once.

What happened to the Jewish priesthood? It fell when the troops of Titus leveled the Herodian Temple in AD 70. Worship for Judaism was now centered in the synagogues and the rabbis. The New Testament, on the other hand, proclaimed a new High Priest and a new kind of priesthood.

The High Priesthood of Jesus
Historically, the church has described Jesus in many ways. Various names have been attributed to Him to describe His

life and ministry. However, the threefold designation of Prophet, Priest, and King has been among the most common. In their confessions of faith, Baptists, like other Christian groups, have used these terms extensively.

No passage in the Bible summarizes this threefold office of Christ any clearer than the prologue to the Book of Hebrews. In this lofty declaration of the theme of Hebrews—the superiority of Christianity to Judaism—the writer says:

In many and various ways God spoke of old to our fathers by the prophets; but in these last days he has spoken to us by a Son, whom he appointed the heir of all things, through whom also he created the world. He reflects the glory of God and bears the very stamp of his nature, upholding the universe by his word of power. When he had made purification for sins, he sat down at the right hand of the Majesty on high, having become as much superior to angels as the name he has obtained is more excellent than theirs (Heb. 1:1-4).

In these verses Christ is portrayed as Prophet, through whom God has spoken His final word (1:1-2); as Priest, who has accomplished a perfect work of cleansing His people's sins (1:3b); and as King, who sits enthroned in the place of chief honor (1:3b).

After my conversion as a freshman in college, one of the first songs I remember singing in the Second Baptist Church of Greenville, Mississippi, was Fanny Crosby's "Praise Him! Praise Him!" The last stanza reflects this emphasis on Christ:

Praise him! praise him! Jesus, our blessed Redeemer!
Heav'nly portals loud with hosannas ring!
Jesus, Savior, reigneth forever and ever;
Crown him! crown him! prophet and priest and King!

Developing his argument throughout the Book of Hebrews, the writer focuses not on the prophet role or kingship of Jesus, but on His priesthood. Indeed, Jesus is the "great high priest" (4:14). He is a "merciful and faithful high priest" (2:17), able to "sympathize with our weaknesses" (4:15). Outside the Levitical line of priesthood (7:11-17), Jesus is a priest "after the order of Melchizedek" (7:11,17), who has opened for us a "new and living way" (10:20) to enter into "the inner shrine behind the curtain" (6:19). The result is revolutionary! Now we can all "draw near to God" (7:19). The writer of Hebrews is intent on demonstrating that Jesus is better than all the priests, sacrifices, and covenants that preceded Him. Christ is the more excellent way.

How? Because Jesus is a superior Priest who offers a superior sacrifice and mediates a superior covenant! The author of Hebrews never uses the word *priesthood* to refer to the early Christians, but it is clear, in light of the practical purpose of the book, that he connects the priesthood of Christ to the continuing life and commitment of the church. In a very real sense, Jesus' priesthood is related to our own. We need to look at three topics: (1) a superior Priest; (2) a superior sacrifice; and (3) His priesthood and ours.

A superior Priest. In what ways is Jesus, as a priest, superior to the Levitical priests under Old Testament law? The writer of the Book of Hebrews answers that question in 4:14-7:28. You would do well to read that passage in its entirety now, because we can look at only two of its emphases.

Jesus' superior priesthood is found in the fact that He was both divine and human. While the old priesthood may have been symbolic of God's presence, Jesus bore "the very stamp of his [God's] nature" (1:3). He was a high priest "without sin" (4:14), "holy, blameless, unstained, separated from sinners, exalted above the heavens" (7:26). Unlike the priests of old, He has no need to offer daily sacrifices for His own sins (7:27). Our priesthood is rooted in Christ, the Great High Priest. He is our basis for hope.

But Jesus is also human. The writer of Hebrews describes this dimension of Jesus' priesthood often and with moving language. Jesus was "made like his brethren in every respect" (2:17). And why? "So that he might become a merciful and faithful high priest in the service of God, to make expiation for the sins of the people" (2:17). He is able to "sympathize with our weaknesses" and "in every respect has been tempted as we are" (4:15). Clarence Jordan makes that verse come alive in his Cotton Patch translation: "We have a leader who isn't coldly indifferent to our weaknesses, but who himself has been put through the mill like we have."[2] Good priesting is impossible without identification. You have to identify with the hurting and the morally bankrupt. We have a model for that!

Jesus' priesthood is superior also because it is not restricted to genealogy or limited by the grave. Jesus is not priest by virtue of Levite origins. He came from the tribe of Judah! Heredity doesn't count! He "belonged to another tribe, from which no one has ever served at the altar" (7:13). Jesus was not recognized as being from a priestly family. He was really a layman. There is your freedom to be a priest! The law that limited priesthood has been "set aside because of its weakness and uselessness" (7:18).

Heredity permitted priesthood under the old covenant. Only death stopped it. But not even death overcame the priestly work of Christ. "He holds his priesthood permanently, because he continues for ever. Consequently he is able for all time to save those who draw near to God through him, since he always lives to make intercession for them" (7:24-25). There is your incentive to keep on priesting; Christ continues His on your behalf.

A superior sacrifice. Including it in a broader discussion of the new covenant (8:1 to 10:18), the author of Hebrews takes pains to describe the superiority of the sacrifice of Christ over that of the old covenant. This description is found in Hebrews 9:1 to 10:18. There is no priesthood without a sacrifice of some kind. That is true of Old Testament priesthood. It is true of your priesthood. It is true of Christ's priesthood. But His sacrifice was different—and superior.

His sacrifice is superior because it is God's one, unrepeatable saving act on our behalf. Unlike the high priest of Israel, who had to offer sacrifice year after year on the Day of Atonement, Jesus entered "once for all into the Holy Place, taking not the blood of goats and calves but his own blood" (9:12). Christ is priest, but He is also victim. "Once for all" he "put away sin by the sacrifice of himself" (9:26). Victim is volunteer. Priests of the old covenant offered the same sacrifices day after day and year after year. "When Christ had offered for all time a single sacrifice for sins, he sat down at the right hand of God" (10:12). He sat down! It did not have to be repeated because it could not be repeated. Nor could it be superseded. This is not a symbol of God's saving act; it is the reality.

Behind all the imagery of sacrifice—so alien to our ears— is a problem with which all priests must deal. It is a problem much older than Aaron, yet as contemporary as your life to-day: guilt and sin. Christ solved it in His priestly work. You and I point to the solution as a part of our priestly act.

One other sign of the superiority of His sacrifice: the curtain has come down! The "Do Not Enter" sign, pinned for centuries to the holy of holies, has come down forever. It now reads: "Everybody welcome." Under the old theology, access is limited. Under the new theology, availability is unlimited. Barrier has become bridge! We—you and I, and everyone who wants to—can come all the way to the throne of grace. Why? Because Jesus has "opened for us" a new way "through the curtain" (10:20). Welcome to the mercy! And welcome to the priesthood! There is no mercy without priesthood, and there is no priesthood without mercy. No wonder that the writer of Hebrews speaks of the sacrifice of Christ as "the time of reformation" (9:10).

PERSONAL LEARNING ACTIVITY 2

Read Hebrews 1:1-4. In the space below, write the words or phrases in these verses that present Jesus as prophet, as priest, and as king.

Prophet: _____

_____

Priest: _____

_____

King: _____

_____

His priesthood and ours. This subject will be echoed again and again throughout this book. The priesthood of believers is implicit in the Book of Hebrews. Hebrews, while profoundly theological, has a very practical purpose. The writer was not merely making an ideological comparison between superior Christianity and inferior Judaism. The Christian recipients of this letter were in a bind of some kind, maybe persecution. Tempted to give up the ship of faith, they are encouraged to persevere (12:1), to lift their drooping hands and strengthen their weak knees (12:12), and not to grow weary or fainthearted (12:3). The writer even describes his letter as a "word of exhortation" (13:22).

A study of the word *therefore* and its equivalents in the letter underlines the writer's intent to exhort (2:1; 3:1,7; 4:1,11,14; 6:1; 9:15; 10:19; 12:1,12; 13:13). He is not primarily a theologian; he is preeminently a preacher. In view of the superior priesthood and superior sacrifice of the Great High Priest, Christians have hope and confidence to fulfill their own calling. Again, the writer never refers explicitly to the people's priesthood, but the concept is implicit throughout the letter.

Hebrews 10:19-25 brings together beautifully this theme of His priesthood and ours. It opens with a "therefore." "Therefore, brethren, since we have confidence to enter the sanctuary by the blood of Jesus, by the new and living way which he opened for us through the curtain, that is, through his flesh, and since we have a great priest over the house of God"—now, how will he conclude? What connection does he make? What follows the "therefore" and the "since"? In light of our newfound "confidence," the new way opened to us, and the "great priest" we cherish, what next?

Here it is, a three-point sermon on the priesthood of the people. "Therefore", he says, "let us draw near with a true heart in full assurance of faith" (10:22). "Therefore," he says, "let us hold fast the confession of our hope without wavering" (10:23). And if that translation doesn't get through, maybe the Cotton Patch will: "Let us hang on with tooth and toenail to our promising commitment."[3] "Therefore," he concludes, "let us consider how to stir up one another to love and good works" (10:24).

"Draw near." "Hold fast." "Stir up." Priestly work for you and me. Even the benediction of Hebrews made the connection between His work and ours:

> Now may the God of peace who brought again from the dead our Lord Jesus, the great shepherd of the sheep, by the blood of the eternal covenant, equip you with everything good that you may do his will, working in you that which is pleasing in his sight, through Jesus Christ; to whom be glory for ever and ever. Amen (13:20-21).

The Priesthood of Believers

Before looking at specific New Testament passages that explicitly teach the doctrine of the priesthood of believers, we need to be mindful of two or three facts. First, Jesus was not a professional priest. In the Gospels Jesus never describes Himself with the designation of "priest." Nor did He ever refer to His disciples as priests or as a priesthood. As we have seen from our study of Hebrews, however, Jesus is certainly perceived by the early church as priestly, even though He lacked the common genealogical credentials.

Second, the phrase *the priesthood of believers* is not found in the Bible. That should not disturb us. The word *Trinity* is not in the Bible either, but the Christian church teaches and believes unquestionably in the doctrine of the Trinity. Clearly, the New Testament, directly and indirectly, teaches not only the high priesthood of Christ, but also the priesthood of Christians.

As you were told in chapter 1, there are five specific references in the New Testament to the priesthood of believers. These are found in two books, 1 Peter and Revelation. Since they are brief, they are printed below so that you can refer to them.

> Like living stones be yourselves built into a spiritual house, to be a holy priesthood, to offer spiritual sacrifices acceptable to God through Jesus Christ (1 Pet. 2:5).

> You are a chosen race, a royal priesthood, a holy nation, God's own people, that you may declare the wonderful

deeds of him who called you out of darkness into his marvelous light (1 Pet. 2:9).

To him who loves us and has freed us from our sins by his blood and made us a kingdom, priests to his God and Father, to him be glory and dominion for ever and ever. Amen (Rev. 1:5-6).

Worthy art thou to take the scroll and to open its seals, for thou wast slain and by thy blood didst ransom men for God from every tribe and tongue and people and nation, and hast made them a kingdom and priests to our God, and they shall reign on earth (Rev. 5:9-10).

Blessed and holy is he who shares in the first resurrection! Over such the second death has no power, but they shall be priests of God and of Christ, and they shall reign with him a thousand years (Rev. 20:6).

Interestingly, 1 Peter and Revelation, along with the Book of Hebrews, are sometimes referred to by New Testament scholars as the literature of persecution. It is an appropriate designation. The Christian recipients of these books are living "under the cross." They are reminded, therefore, of who and whose they are, how they should conduct themselves, and what they are called to do. Each of these five passages deserves individual attention in light of its separate background. However, we need only to identify some major themes issuing from the five references as a group.

Identification of the priesthood. Just who are the priests in these passages? The ordained? The clergy? Church staff? Those who have been in the church for years? The theologically literate? Look! They come "from every tribe," not just Levi. They come from every "tongue and people and nation" (Rev. 5:9); God has made them all priests. Who are they? They are those who have been called "out of darkness" (1 Pet. 2:9), freed from sins (Rev. 1:5), and ransomed from the slave block (Rev. 5:9). The priests are "yourselves" (1 Pet. 2:5), "you" (1 Pet. 2:9), and "us" (Rev. 1:5). The only certification for priesthood is salvation. Here it is again: there is no mercy without priesthood! Priesthood comes with pardon. When we ask the unbeliever, Do you want to be a Christian? we are also asking, Do you want to be a priest?

It is clear from 1 Peter 2:5 that first-century Christians based their case for an inclusive priesthood directly on Exodus 19:6 and to a lesser degree on Isaiah 61:6, verses quoted at the beginning of the chapter. Why is this fact significant? Simply because hundreds of references in the Old Testament to a "special" and "professional" priesthood were intentionally ignored. Christians selected these two passages, almost unique in the Old Testament, which designate all the people of God as priests. For the church, all Christians, not a select few, are ordained to the priesthood. Priesthood includes both laity and clergy. Privilege and responsibility are equally distributed among all Christians. And that is why we call it the *universal* priesthood of believers.[4]

All are priests. But all are priests "through Jesus Christ" (1 Pet. 2:5). Read carefully all five passages and you will see the Christological focus. Christ is the one who has called us out of darkness, freed us from our sins, and ransomed us by His blood. Here it is again: there is no priesthood without mercy! We are priests "of Christ" (Rev. 20:6). "We are not just *a* priestly body, as in Israel; we are *his* priestly body offered afresh in obedience to God and in compassion for men."[5] Christian priesthood is not priesthood in general. That is why we call it the priesthood of *believers*.

Character of the priesthood. Two characteristics of the priesthood of believers dominate these passages. First, Christians constitute a "holy" priesthood (1 Pet. 2:5) and a "holy" nation (1 Pet. 2:9). These two verses in 1 Peter are placed within a lengthier passage (1 Pet. 1:13 to 2:10), in which the writer appeals to persecuted Christians to remember whose they are. "As he who called you is holy, be holy yourselves in all your conduct," Peter says in 1:15. Their model for holiness is none other than God. Holiness, however, is not simply a self-righteous preoccupation with one's personal life. *Holiness* means Christian maturity expressed in "a sincere love of the brethren" (1 Pet. 1:22). Holiness is not haughtiness. Holiness is love for people. Therefore, we are to "put away all malice and all guile and insincerity and envy and all slander" (1 Pet. 2:1). Holy people are loving people.

Years ago I heard an evangelist say something I have never forgotten. In giving his personal testimony, he said, "God found me in the middle of nothing, set me in the middle of everything, and gave me such a heavenly jerk that I have been out of joint with the world ever since." Was he bragging, holding himself up as a standard for the rest of us? To be honest, I thought so. But in ways far deeper than we usually apply it, Christians are indeed to be "out of joint with the world." Here are some questions for gauging your holiness: Will you welcome all Christians, regardless of race, into your church? Do you believe your gender is superior to the other? Do you abuse your spouse and children—verbally? How do you spend your money in light of a hungry and hurting world? What do your check stubs say about "loving the brethren"? The way of holiness is a hard way. It is, nonetheless, the way of Christian priesthood.

Second, Christians are a "royal" priesthood (1 Pet. 2:9). Christians belong to a King who has a kingdom. We are kingdom priests (Rev. 1:6). Every citizen-priest can approach the King, and every citizen-priest should reflect the character of the kingdom. And this is a kingdom with new values, new methods, and new goals. But this is not a kingdom that we build. We can receive it and enter it. We can and must proclaim it. We serve or "priest" in this kingdom, where we are "priests of God and of Christ" (Rev. 20:6). The Christian priest is a willing servant under God's sovereignty.

But there is more. This royal priesthood will also reign with the King (Rev. 5:10; 20:6). Remember the circumstances! Christians are receiving this word about reigning in a time of persecution. Here is a triumphantly encouraging word for priests in a pinch. When the church appeared to be an insignificant community and the hand of the Roman emperor was coming down hard—just at that moment came the message about their own royalty and reign.

But "the amazing paradox," as Frank Stagg says, "is that man reigns with Christ precisely when he gives up all notions of reigning."[6] When you seek to reign, you become a slave to your own power and ambition. When you willingly serve, when you are more concerned with priesting than reigning, then comes the privilege of the reign.

Vocation of the priesthood. What is the work of the Christian priesthood? The Old Testament priests served the dual roles of intercession and interpretation. They were mediators who brought the people to God in worship; they were teachers who brought the word of God to the people. Something of this same pattern of priestly function appears in our five New Testament passages. The calling of the priesthood of believers is to worship and to witness. Priests must face God in praise and the world in service. They do their work on a two-way street.

Priests worship. They relate to God. Thus, the passages in Revelation reflect a people of praise. "To him be glory and dominion for ever and ever. Amen" (Rev. 1:6) and "worthy art thou" (Rev. 5:9) are doxological. That is, they speak praise. The setting is that of worship, and it speaks of the privilege of priesthood.

A priest who doesn't worship is as inconceivable as a doctor who doesn't heal, a teacher who doesn't teach, or a truck driver who doesn't drive. It is a contradiction of terms. Through Christ, admonished the writer of Hebrews, "let us continually offer up a sacrifice of praise to God, that is, the fruit of lips that acknowledge his name" (Heb. 13:15).

Worship is both personal and communal. Both dimensions are important. The references in the Revelation passages, however, are clearly to a *community* at worship. One of the first telltale signs that something has gone wrong in the life of a believer is abstinence from corporate worship. Priesthood implies meeting other priests to offer up sacrifices of praise.

Priests also witness. They act for God in the world. "You are . . . a royal priesthood . . . God's own people, that you may declare the wonderful deeds of him who called you out of darkness into his marvelous light" (1 Pet. 2:9) speaks of missions. The setting is that of the world of work and home, and it speaks of the responsibility of priesthood.

A priest who restricts his role to the altar is as ineffective as one who never approached the altar. "God so loved the world. . . !" "Go into all the world. . . !" T. W. Manson interpreted the history of the church correctly: "The Christianity that conquered the Roman Empire was not an affair of brilliant preachers addressing packed congregations."[7] But Carlyle Marney said it much better: ". . . the church has to get out of the house."[8]

Why? To be priests! To declare His wonderful deeds! How? By word spoken and by life lived. We should not be surprised, therefore, that the writer of Hebrews followed doxology with a call to missions. After encouraging his readers to "continually offer up a sacrifice of praise to God," he said, "Do not neglect to do good and to share what you have, for such sacrifices are pleasing to God" (Heb. 13:16). The sacrifice of praise and the sacrifice of service! That is the work of the priesthood of believers.

PERSONAL LEARNING ACTIVITY 3
As priests of God, we are called to worship and witness. Why is worship an important responsibility for the Christian?

Why is witnessing a responsibility for the Christian?

Notes

1. William E. Hull, "The New Testament Concept of the Priesthood of the Believer," *Search,* Winter 1972, 6.
2. Reprinted from THE COTTON PATCH VERSION OF HEBREWS AND THE GENERAL EPISTLES by Clarence Jordan copyright 1973 by Florence Jordan, by permission of New Century Publishers, Inc., Piscataway, New Jersey, 25.
3. Ibid., 34.
4. Hull, 9.
5. Hull, 10.
6. Frank Stagg, *New Testament Theology* (Nashville: Broadman Press, 1962), 166.
7. T. W. Manson, *Ministry and Priesthood: Christ's and Ours* (Richmond: John Knox Press, n.d.), 21.
8. Carlyle Marney, *Priests to Each Other* (Valley Forge: The Judson Press, 1974), 13. Used by permission of Judson Press.

Chapter 3
The Priesthood of Believers and Salvation

While I was a student at New Orleans Baptist Theological Seminary, the late Carlyle Marney lectured on our campus. In a chapel address, he gave us vintage Marney! His address was overlaid with so many historical allusions, so many poetic images, so many profound thoughts wrapped in such mysterious language that we all left talking about how great it was, while not a half dozen of us, including the faculty, really knew what he had said.

Immediately after the chapel service, Marney appeared in one of the theology classes to answer questions about his address. The first fellow to his feet was a first-year student who hadn't been at seminary long enough to be "cool" and hide his ignorance like the rest of us. He blurted out: "Dr. Marney, I heard you in chapel a few minutes ago, and frankly I didn't understand a word you said. Can you tell me in simple language what the gospel of Jesus Christ really is?" Marney paused, peered over his glasses, and stared the Grand Canyon into the fellow. Then he turned, walked to the chalkboard, picked up a piece of chalk, and after waiting an interminable moment, wrote four words on the board in capitals: GOD IS FOR *YOU!* And he underlined *you.*

Marney was right. The gospel of Jesus Christ is for *you* as an individual. And that is where the priesthood of believers begins. For a study of the doctrine of salvation, the priesthood of believers means that *the individual cannot be denied.* Salvation is exceedingly personal. It requires the response of the individual.

In the Greek New Testament the word for *salvation* is *soteria.* When theologians study soteriology, they are studying the doctrine of salvation. The root meaning of *soteria* is health and wholeness. Health is needed for sickness or disease. Wholeness is needed for fragmentation and separation. Something has gone terribly wrong! Humanity is sick with the disease of sin. People are fragmented, torn apart, and separated from the very Source of life. Although sin has momentous social implications and manifestations, it is first and foremost personal. Sin requires a personal cure and personal wholeness. It mandates personal salvation.

What is the significance of the priesthood of believers for salvation? Here it is: *the privilege of uncoerced personal ac-*

cess to God's grace for your sin. God is for *you!* We shall look at salvation in light of the priesthood of believers from three directions: (1) the equality of access to salvation; (2) the personal nature of grace; and (3) the voluntary nature of faith.

The equality of access to salvation. In his book *The Axioms of Religion,* which has been so popular among Southern Baptists, E. Y. Mullins identified equal access to God as the "religious axiom." An axiom is a self-evident truth, and in this case, the religious axiom "asserts the inalienable right of every soul to deal with God for itself."[1] Mullins went on to point out that this axiom implies the human capacity to commune with God. "It denies that there are any barriers to any soul to any part of the Father's grace," and it affirms that "all have equal access to the Father's table, the Father's ear, and the Father's heart."[2] Moreover, Mullins argued, to deprive any person of the privilege of direct access to God is nothing less than "tyranny." Mullins also made the point, which I shall make in a later chapter, that this axiom expresses itself in the individual's right to read, study, and interpret the Scriptures.

Equality of access to God's grace for salvation is not rooted in human capability. It is based firmly on God's sovereignty. It means that God's sovereignty is not relinquished. John D. Freeman, you remember, called this "the undelegated sovereignty of Christ." Before Christ alone the individual must stand or fall. Equal access does not mean that people save themselves. Salvation is God's act, completely and solely. It is God's initiative.

Paul made this crystal clear in his often quoted passage in Ephesians 2:8-9: "By grace you have been saved through faith; and this is not your own doing, it is the gift of God—not because of works, lest any man should boast." "He saved us," said Paul in another place, "not because of deeds done by us in righteousness, but in virtue of his own mercy, by the washing of regeneration and renewal in the Holy Spirit, which he poured out upon us richly through Jesus Christ our Savior" (Titus 3:5-6). So whatever else the priesthood of believers suggests, it does not even hint at the idea that each priest is saved by his or her own works.

Salvation, therefore, is God's act on behalf of our helplessness. But God's act is on behalf of *all* people, who have *equal access* to God through Christ Jesus. This point was made repeatedly in chapter 2 as we examined the Book of Hebrews. In the New Testament, however, this emphasis is not restricted to Hebrews.

In the incarnation, God demonstrated equality of access in the life and actions of Jesus. All four Gospels portray Jesus as available not to a select few, but to all who would come to Him (Matt. 11:28). His posture is inclusive, not exclusive. He set the pattern for His approach in His inaugural sermon at Nazareth (Luke 4:16-30). From their own Scriptures, the Jews are told by Christ that Gentiles are included. And a Gentile leper—one considered unclean—at that!

John's Gospel (chap. 4) tells the beautiful story of Jesus' openness to a Samaritan woman with a morally bankrupt background. A Samaritan! A woman! A sinner! None of these classifications constituted a barrier for Christ, although they did for others of His day. John closed the story with an affirmation from "many Samaritans" who exclaimed, "This is indeed the Savior of the world" (John 4:42). And later in John's Gospel, after some Greeks had come to Him, Jesus said, "I, when I am lifted up from the earth, will draw all men to myself" (John 12:32).

Possibly no passage from the New Testament describes the theme of equal access to God any better or more graphically than Ephesians 2:11-22. And maybe no Southern Baptist theologian has dealt with the passage more extensively or thoroughly than has Dr. William E. Hull. In *Beyond the Barriers,* a book that deserves a wide reading audience among Southern Baptists, published in 1981 by Broadman Press, Hull explores the theme of reconciliation and its meaning for the contemporary church. This book deals with some important truths that all serious Christians would do well to consider.

In this book Hull deals with Ephesians 2:11-22. It is a lengthy passage, too long to reproduce here. Let me encourage you, therefore, to read the passage from your Bible a couple of times before proceeding with this study.

Hull contends, and rightly so, that the context for understanding this passage was the Jewish Temple in Jerusalem where the priests did their work. In verse 14 Paul speaks of a "dividing wall." In contrast, in verses 19-22 he speaks of a structure which is "joined together" and which becomes "a holy temple." The temple motif dominates the passage, and Paul used it to contrast the difference between the Jewish religion and the Christian faith.

"The Temple in Jerusalem was a parable in stone of the Jewish approach to God."[3] It was theology in architecture. Built into it were both inequality and inaccessibility. The Temple included a building and four courtyards. Only the priests entered the building and only the high priest entered the small chamber, called the holy of holies, within the building. The people worshiped in the outer four courtyards, which were carefully separated by walls. The first courtyard was the Court of the Gentiles. They could go no farther! The second was the Court of Women. They could go no farther! The third was the Court of Israel. Jewish males could go no farther! The fourth was the Court of Priests. And although they could enter the outer part of the building, they could go no farther! Only the high priest could enter the holy of holies but, as we have seen, only once a year.

Separating the courtyards were "walls" that "were not merely decorative but were determinative of Israel's basic understanding of the nature of religion. They did not serve simply to organize available space in convenient fashion; instead, they literally put each person in his or her proper place in relation both to others and to God."[4]

Back to Ephesians 2:11-22. What is Paul's point in this passage? Simple: Jesus Christ brought the walls down! Jesus is a new kind of Joshua, bringing down the walls of inaccessibility to God. He came and preached peace to those who were far off and those who were near. The result? "Through him we both have access in one Spirit to the Father" (2:18). In chapter 3 of Ephesians Paul follows this with a statement about God's "eternal purpose," which has been realized in Christ Jesus, "in whom we have boldness and confidence of access through our faith" (Eph. 3:12). Inaccessibility to God always results in inequality among people. On the other hand, accessibility to God leads to equality among believers—Jew and Gentile, male and female, priest and laity, and big priest and small priest (see Gal. 3:28 and Col. 3:11).

D. T. Niles, in a masterful paragraph, demonstrates the relationship between accessibility to God and equality among people. Speaking of Christ, Niles said:

> We see how he broke down every single barrier that existed in his day between man and man, and interest and interest. He enlisted Simon the Zealot as a disciple, setting aside political distinction. (Luke 6:15.) He dined with Zacchaeus, setting aside class distinction. (Luke 19:5.) He conversed with the woman of Samaria, setting aside sex distinction. (John 4:27.) He responded to the appeal of the Syrophoenician woman, setting aside race distinction. (Mark 7:26.) He extolled the faith of the Centurion, setting aside national distinction. (Matt. 8:10.) He befriended sinners, setting aside popular distinction. (Matt. 11:19.) He allowed the woman who was a sinner to touch him, setting aside reputational distinction. (Luke 7:39.) He praised the poor widow who gave her mite, setting aside economic distinction. (Mark 12:43.) He washed his disciples' feet, setting aside the master-servant distinction. (John 13:14.) He rebuked his disciples for their intolerance toward that follower who was not of the twelve, setting aside denominational distinction. (Mark 9:39.) He enjoyed the company of children, setting aside age distinction. (Mark 21:15.) His was a barrierless love.[5]

Speaking of Christ in this same vein, Paul says, "He is our peace, who has made us both one, and has broken down the dividing wall of hostility" (Eph. 2:14). When a wall falls one way, people can go two ways—both to God and to one another.

The falling walls of the Jerusalem Temple gave way to a new "structure." This structure has no "strangers" and "sojourners," only "fellow citizens," "members of the household of God." Christ is the "cornerstone" of this new building. In Him the whole structure is "joined together" and becomes "a dwelling place of God." Equality has replaced inequality; accessibility has replaced inaccessibility.

Equality of access to grace is necessary for several reasons, not the least of which is the fact, as we have just seen, that such is the way God has ordered things. Also, equal accessibility is available because equal accountability is inevitable (Rom. 14:12). Moreover, equality of access is needful because inequality of access fosters an impersonal and proxy relationship to God. To that general subject, we must now turn.

The personal nature of grace. What is the essence of God's grace in our salvation? Is it legalistic? Do we have a law to keep? Is it ritualistic? Do we have cultic acts to perform? Is it creedalistic? Do we have doctrines to which we must assent? Again, what is the significance of the priesthood of believers for salvation? It is the privilege of uncoerced *personal* access to God's grace for our sin. Salvation is personal, relational, and individualistic; else, it is no salvation at all.

God's intervention in history on our behalf was personal and relational. "The Word became flesh and dwelt among us, full of grace and truth; we have beheld his glory, glory as of the only Son from the Father" (John 1:14). "Flesh!" That's personal. "Dwelt among us"—personally. "Son . . . Father!" That's relational. "His name shall be called Emmanuel" (Matt. 1:23). *Emmanuel* translates as *God with us.* God did not save us by writing an impersonal note in the sky or by sending us a systematic theology book to read. He saved us by sending His Son to earth.

> That which was from the beginning, which we have heard, which we have seen with our eyes, which we have looked upon and touched with our hands, concerning the word of life—the life was made manifest, and we saw it, and testify to it, and proclaim to you the eternal life which was with the Father and was made manifest to us—that which we have seen and heard we proclaim also to you, so that you may have fellowship with us; and our fellowship is with the Father and with his Son Jesus Christ (1 John 1:1-3).

Some heresies die hard. One of the earliest that Christians faced has continued through the years under various names. It was gnosticism. The passage from 1 John intended to refute this heresy. What did gnosticism teach? Many things, but only two ideas are pertinent. Gnosticism taught that matter is evil, that only spirit is good. Therefore, Christ was not really human; He only appeared to be human. It is an impersonal and overly spiritualized understanding of the incarnation of God in Christ. So John insisted that Jesus was a real person whom he had heard with his own ears, seen with his own eyes, and touched with his own hands. In falsely spiritualizing Jesus, Gnostics impersonalized Him. Second, Gnostics claimed that salvation came through secret knowledge. The word *gnostic* comes from the Greek word *gnosis,* which means *knowledge.* The apostle John, however, did not speak of salvation as secret doctrine; he spoke of it in personal terms—"fellowship . . . with the Father and with his Son." We are not saved by *gnosis.* We are saved by a personal Savior!

And we are saved one by one, person by person, and individual by individual. No effort here to minimize community! The theme of the *individual in community* is a cardinal biblical theme, present in both Old and New Testaments. But salvation is not church by church, community by community, or nation by nation. It is lonely soul by lonely soul.

Just as access to grace is equal, it is also agonizingly personal. Jeremiah preached this point six hundred years before Christ. In what has been called "the gospel before the gospel," Jeremiah promised the coming of a new covenant. This is what Jeremiah said that God said about the coming covenant: "I will put my law within them, and I will write it upon their hearts" (Jer. 31:33). God would take pen in hand and write not on stone but on the inner being of the individual, prophesied Jeremiah. "They shall all know me," God said, "from the least of them to the greatest" (Jer. 31:34). "To *know* God is not a formal affair, but a direct, dynamic, intimate, personal fellowship with God which controls the course of one's life. This does not come through creed and ceremony but through contact and communion."[6] Jeremiah's prophecy of the new covenant is so important for first-century Christians that the writer of Hebrews quoted it not once but twice in a space of two chapters (see Heb. 8:8-12; 10:16-17).

A communal priesthood of believers does not exist without personal mercy for the individual priests. That is why Martin

Luther based his doctrine of the priesthood of believers on the theological principle of justification by faith. Why do we try to add something to grace? Why can't we let it be? Why, through the centuries, have we resented it so much for ourselves and for others? Maybe we cannot keep our hands off it because we are so accustomed to bad news that we cannot hear good news. Watch what we do with the personal, individual grace of God.

We try to substitute for it. We want to send someone else to get it for us. There are no surrogates for a personal encounter. You can't send another priest to bring God's grace to you. The church does not bring God's grace to us. Certainly Jesus "came to create a new people of God [community], but he went about it by addressing individual persons: James and John, Andrew and Peter, Matthew the taxgatherer, and many others."[7] Do you see why E. Y. Mullins called this "the principle of individualism in religion"?[8] Try as we may, we cannot send a proxy for the grace that saves us as individuals.

Nor can we add to God's grace. But ever since the Judaizers in the first century, we have tried to add something to personal grace and individual faith. The church has never been able to rid itself of what Paul called "the circumcision party" (Gal. 2:12). Judaizers were Jewish Christians unable to believe grace alone, so they attempted to add the law, especially circumcision, as a requirement for salvation. Paul fought them at every turn, calling them what they were— perverters of the gospel of Christ (Gal. 1:7).

The central issue in the Book of Galatians is: What makes a Christian a Christian? Paul's repetitive answer is singular— faith in Christ (Gal. 2:15-16,20; 3:26; 5:6). And although Jesus was a faithful Jew, there is "not a trace in all his recorded words of any advocacy of circumcision."[9] He shifted the entire understanding of religion away from law keeping, physical ancestry, or national identification and turned it toward personal faith and individual discipleship.

The temptation to add to the gospel of God's grace for the individual pervades all denominations. Some add baptism. Some add the Lord's Supper. Some add this creed or that doctrine. It is "the circumcision party" all over again. If not corrected, the gospel of grace is perverted. There is nothing to add! Personal faith in Christ Jesus is sufficient!

Some substitute. Some add. But some subtract in an effort to find a personal relationship to God. In his letter to the Colossians Paul confronted a heresy different from the Judaizers. The Colossian distortion suggested that salvation came "in promoting rigor of devotion and self-abasement and severity to the body" (Col. 2:23). Their line was "'Do not handle, Do not taste, Do not touch'" (2:21). This is an effort at salvation by negation.

Self-denial is at the heart of Jesus' call to salvation. There is a world of difference, however, between denying things to yourself and denying yourself. "Surely there is a place for pruning the branch. . . . But pruning a branch can only be effective if the branch is already in touch with the vine."[10] Salvation by subtraction is only another way of impersonalizing our individual relationship to God. It does not work.

Nor does multiplication. Some replace individual grace with individual works. We are "created in Christ Jesus for good works" (Eph. 2:10), but we are not created in Christ Jesus *by* good works. God's creation does not come to us by attending three more committee meetings or giving an extra one hundred dollars. We have to relate personally to God and receive forgiveness individually from Him. The opposite of *sin* in the Bible is not *goodness;* it is *grace.*

So, our scheming for salvation is fruitless. Substitution, addition, subtraction, and multiplication—all are efforts at avoiding the meeting. Again, why do we fear it so? Where is the threat in personal access to grace? The threat is in the grace itself. I know, and you do too, why many people would rather be saved by law than by grace, if they could. That way they earn it! That way they achieve it! In this world, as we have been told all our lives, you don't get something for nothing; you've got to earn it. We fear personal grace because we fear indebtedness. We do not want to be overtaken by something we cannot control.

If we resist grace for ourselves, it is certainly no surprise that we resent it for others even more. If we don't want to be saved by grace, we surely do not want to live by grace. Just as the Pharisees objected to Jesus' receiving sinners and eating with them, the elder son resented the father's celebration for the scoundrel son (Luke 15:25-30). You see, this church-going, faithful-to-his-family, moral bookkeeping older brother wanted something other than grace for his younger brother. He wanted justice! In this world, you don't get something for nothing, he thought.

Enter the father! Enter the personal relationship! And justice becomes grace. Maybe it is the personal, individual nature of that grace that we fear the most. The threat of salvation is that we cannot find it hiding in a group or mass of people. We have to come out of the crowd alone and go "before God." Let those two words rest on your soul slowly. "Before God!" "*Before* God!" "Before *God*!" *"Before God!"* There is the threat and the resistance. But it is the only way to grace. It is the only way to priesthood. It is the way of individualism.

Critics often take on this dimension of the priesthood of believers with ridicule. They pronounce it an extreme, rugged, and unbridled individualism. Let them rail! W. R. White was right to include a chapter on "The Primacy of the Individual" in his book titled *Baptist Distinctives.* E. Y. Mullins was right to speak of "The Principle of Individualism in Religion" in *The Axioms of Religion.* Both White and Mullins stand in the Baptist and the biblical traditions.

To emphasize individualism is not to deny community. It is a way of saying that salvation grace is personal. You cannot say everything at one time, especially when a truth is bifocal. Individualism is only half the story, but without it, the whole story cannot be told. Individualism in salvation is where the doctrine of the priesthood of believers begins. It is not where it ends.

PERSONAL LEARNING ACTIVITY 4
This chapter speaks of ways that people avoid the truth of the gospel by substitution, subtraction, and multiplication. Read this material carefully; then give an example of each.

1. Some try to substitute for the gospel by _____

_____

2. Some attempt to add to the gospel by _____

3. Some subtract from the gospel by _____

_____

4. Some try to multiply the gospel by _____

_____

The voluntary nature of faith. Salvation is like a coin; it has two sides. On one side is God's grace. That grace, we have said, is accessible to all and exceedingly personal in nature. On the other side of the coin is a person's faith. That faith is voluntary. No one is forced to believe because no one can be forced to believe. Faith is an act of the human will, just as grace is an act of the sovereignty of God.

Another way of saying this is to underline the truth that our priesthood is an act of choice. If we choose God's grace for our lives by faith, we also choose to be Christian priests. Priesthood is not coerced upon us, because salvation is a choice we make. Christian priests are not born priests, as were the Levitical priests in the Old Testament. We don't inherit priesthood any more than we inherit salvation. When we choose the mercy of God by faith, we also choose to be a priest. Again, that is not only biblical but also Baptist.

Martin E. Marty, a Lutheran, and America's best-known and foremost church historian, has made the point that choice is at the heart of the Baptist faith. In the September 2, 1983, issue of *Christianity Today,* Marty wrote an intriguing article titled "Baptistification Takes Over." Marty's made-up word is awkward, he admits, but he created it to describe what he called "the most dramatic shift in power style on the Christian scene in our time."

What does he mean by "baptistification" and by "dramatic shift"? Let me tell you first what he does not mean. To baptistify is not to lead persons to unite only with Baptist churches. One can be baptistified and be a Catholic, Anglican, or Lutheran, Marty says. Nor does *baptistify* mean to baptize. He refers to a mood among such groups as Catholics, Lutherans, and Anglicans to stress freedom, choice, and voluntarism in matters of faith. Marty correctly argues that these characteristics are hallmarks of the Baptist identity. The emphasis is on the decisional dimension of faith.

Marty is saying that a "dramatic shift" is occurring in Christendom from having decisions made for oneself to freedom to choose for oneself. The point to take note of is that America's finest church historian, who thoroughly understands who Baptists are, knows that the voluntary nature of faith is crucial to our denominational identity. This is part of what E. Y. Mullins meant by "soul competency."

John Cuddy works across the street from the First Baptist Church in Macon, Georgia. He is the Roman Catholic priest at St. Joseph's Catholic Church and one of the most respected ministers in our city. We had him over to First Baptist one Wednesday night to tell us what Catholics believe. Near the end of the session I asked him, "Father Cuddy, what one thing do you admire most about Baptists?" Without struggling for an answer, he answered quickly and with one word: "Freedom." He nailed us! He did not elaborate, and he could have meant several things—the freedom of Baptists to read and interpret the Bible for themselves, the freedom of Baptists to order their church life without external interference, or the freedom from creeds or from the state. But he could also have meant the freedom to choose to believe. It is at the heart of the Baptist genius.

It is at the heart of the Baptist genius because we believe it is at the heart of the Bible. From Genesis to Revelation, human beings are portrayed as free to believe or disbelieve, to follow or to turn away. In the Old Testament God gave Himself to Israel in a covenant relationship. This was no bilateral covenant in which each party of the covenant decided what was to be included. This was a unilateral covenant. God determined the nature of the covenant. God offered the covenant. This is God's sovereignty. But God did not impose the covenant. It was not crammed down the soul of Israel. Israel received the covenant, agreed to the covenant, and chose the covenant. That is human freedom. Israel can accept or reject the covenant; Israel could not alter the covenant: " 'All that the Lord has spoken we will do'" (Ex. 19:8).

Maybe no incident in the life of Jesus reflects the freedom to choose as does the story of the lame man in John 5:1-9. "One man was there," John says, "who had been ill for thirty-eight years." When Jesus saw him and knew that he had been lying there for a long time, He said to him, "'Do you want to be healed?'" While the question may strike you as strange, aren't you aware of people who preferred their sickness to health? Jesus gave a choice—disease or deliverance. It reminds me of a picture I saw hanging on an office wall in the Richmond, Virginia, airport. At the top was a very fat little boy staring regretfully at himself in a full-length mirror. In the middle was another picture of the same boy, running and sweating. A book was beside him, and it was titled *How to Jog.* The caption at the bottom of the picture read: "Tomorrow can be better than today. It is up to us!"

The prodigal son realized that, too (Luke 15:11-24). According to Jesus, this boy had an incredible father. And the father gave incredible freedom. He gave his son the freedom to walk out, leave home, and live a rebel's life. Isn't one of the most awesome things about life the fact that God leaves the front gate open? He will let us take our lives into our own hands and make a colossal mess of things. But that's only the beginning of the story.

He also gave the son the freedom to return after the mess was made. You have observed before, haven't you, that Luke 15 contains three stories of lost things? In the first story a shepherd has lost a sheep. In the second story a woman has lost a coin. In the last a father with two sons has lost one son. Did you observe that in the first story the shepherd goes after the sheep and brings it back to the fold? And in the second story Jesus described in minute detail how the woman sweeps the house clean, searching for the coin until she finds it. But there is no description of the father going after the son. He is the waiting father.

Do you know why? Because you can put a little sheep on your shoulder, and *force* it to come home. And you can take an inanimate coin and place it back where it belongs. Coins have no will. But there is not a father in this world who, finding a lost son, can force him back home to stay.

Some words simply cannot be put together. "Forced love!" There is no such thing. You can force labor. You can force slavery. But you cannot force love. So the father leaves the front gate open. You are free to leave. You are free to return. All of us have left. The only choice before us now is whether to return or to stay gone. But we do not have the choice of not choosing. To refuse to choose is to choose to stay away. However, the choice is ours. Faith is always voluntary.

What does all this freedom mean? How do we Baptists translate it? We translate it into conversion by conviction, not conversion by compulsion. We translate it into priesthood by choice, not priesthood by birth or force. We translate it into evangelism by persuasion, not evangelism by manipulation. We translate it into believer's baptism, anti-creedalism, congregationalism, religious liberty, individual interpretation of the Bible, and separation of church and state. The voluntary nature of faith says much about our priesthood—in salvation and in other areas of our discipleship.

PERSONAL LEARNING ACTIVITY 5

On a separate sheet, write a brief account of your conversion experience. Be sure to emphasize the role of personal choice in your decision.

Notes

1. E. Y. Mullins, *The Axioms of Religion* (Philadelphia: The Judson Press, 1908), 92.
2. Ibid.
3. William E. Hull, *Beyond the Barriers* (Nashville: Broadman Press, 1981), 26-27.
4. Ibid., 28.
5. D. T. Niles, *That They May Have Life* (New York: Harper & Row, 1951), 44-45. Used by permission.
6. James Leo Green, "Jeremiah," *The Broadman Bible Commentary,* Volume 6, ed. Clifton J. Allen (Nashville: Broadman Press, 1971), 153.
7. Reprinted from POLARITIES OF MAN'S EXISTENCE IN BIBLICAL PERSPECTIVE, by Frank Stagg. Copyright © MCMLXXIII The Westminster Press, 79. Reprinted and used by permission.
8. Mullins, 93.
9. Hull, 44.
10. Ernest T. Campbell, "Saved by Grace," 4. A sermon preached by Campbell at the Riverside Church in New York City, March 16, 1973.

Chapter 4
The Priesthood of Believers and the Church

The doctrine of the priesthood of believers says that the individual cannot be denied salvation. As I said in chapter 3, that is only half the story. Without it, however, the whole story cannot be told. The other half of the story relates to the church, the priestly community. And what does the priesthood of believers affirm, explicitly and implicitly, for the church? It affirms that the community cannot be ignored.

While the priesthood of believers affirms important truths for the individual, it is not spiritual lone rangerism. The priesthood of believers is not a sophisticated phrase for the folk theology stating that "every tub sits on its own bottom." Those five priesthood passages in 1 Peter and Revelation address the issue of community more than the idea of unrestrained individualism. True! The individual cannot be slaughtered. Also true! The community must not be butchered into tiny slices. Critics not only have a point, but they also have a legitimate, biblical reason to excoriate any emphasis that overlooks the corporate nature of the Christian priesthood. So Paul D. Hanson was safe to write a brilliant book titled *The People Called: the Growth of Community in the Bible.*

The story line of the Bible is not the heroic achievements of isolated individuals. Abraham, Moses, David, Jeremiah, Peter, and Paul are not pictured in holy Scripture as invincible individualists who, in their isolation, whipped the forces of evil. They are portrayed as people in community, aware of historical identity and treasured traditions and in need of the genuine values of relationships.

Where does all this lead? To a repudiation of individualism in salvation? No! To a rebuke of the often heard excuse "I don't need the church; I can do my business with God on the golf course or on the lake as well as I can with the church"? Yes! And stern rebuke at that! Bluntly, your business with God is not simply *your* business. It is God's business, and God's business is far bigger than merely to walk with *you* and to talk with *you* and to tell *you* that *you* are His own. God's business has, as I tried to say in chapter 3, very much to do with *you*, but it has to do with you *in community.*

Indeed, one of the major problems of contemporary American Christianity is the way the "electronic church," as well as some parachurch movements, undercuts the role of community in church life. In time, we must, and I think we shall, relearn the difference between a clientele and a congregation. Richard John Neuhaus is right in saying that "thousands of pulpit entrepreneurs and multimillion dollar 'Christian networks' thrive on the selling of a Christianity that is divorced from, even posited against, Christian community."[1] We have lived, says Neuhaus, to see the emergence of "solid-state spirituality that centers on TV tube and cassette." Many radio and TV ministries are helpful, but too often this type of spirituality is perpetuated by authoritarian personalities who, however unwittingly, play havoc with both the communal and the personal aspects of the priesthood of believers.

A saint in our church possesses a better instinct. Elderly and ill, she is unable to meet with First Baptist Church in Macon, Georgia, for regular worship. So every Sunday morning she gets the order of worship that is included in our newsletter (a good practice for a number of reasons), turns on her radio to the broadcast of our worship service, and worships at her bedside. She told me, "I follow the worship service, sing, or hum the hymns along with the congregation, pray when they pray, read God's Word with them—just as if I were in the sanctuary at the top of Poplar Street." With a hunger for community so pervasive in the Bible, she adds, "It makes me feel I belong!" I looked her straight in the eyes and told her the truth, "You do!" Community cannot be ignored. Any doctrine of the priesthood of believers that says otherwise has tortured the meaning of priesthood.

Whose Church Is This?

How do you answer? The question is not only relevant; it is also necessary if we plumb the depths of what the priesthood of believers means for the doctrine of the church. Fred Jones served as chairman of the committee that delivered me as pastor to that priceless priesthood at First Baptist Church in Ruston, Louisiana. Prior to that congregational call, Fred, with his judgelike wisdom and diabolical humor, warned, "Walter, you will probably get some negative votes, but don't take it personally; they will probably be directed at me rather than you." Then he added, "Some people in Ruston contend that FBC stands for Fred's Baptist Church!" Fred Jones launched me in more ways than I can say grace over, but of this one thing I am sure. He engaged me with the question, Whose church is this? Fred's critics, I have concluded, were mostly wrong but partially right, and in the process of their criticism, they overlooked some things.

Well, whose is it? Whose church is this? The answers are found from Genesis to Revelation, but the focal point is Ephesians, especially chapters 2 and 3.

This is God's church! Here is the first answer. It is first not only in order, but also in importance. Every other answer is subordinate and secondary. If first you answer the question in any other way, you fail the exam.

The English word *church* is related to the Greek word *ekklesia.* In pagan Greek usage the term meant *to call* or *to call out,* and it is used to designate an assembly of some kind. The primary antecedent of the New Testament usage, however, is not in the Greek meaning but in the theology of the Old Testament. The Hebrew words *qahal* and *edah* describe the people of God, whether assembled or otherwise. The emphasis is on the possessive—the Lord's people. The stress is not on the ones called but on the one who calls. Saints are certainly called out, but in the New Testament the primary emphasis of the term *the ekklesia of God* is on the caller.

Ownership belongs to God. Thus, Paul in Ephesians 2:19 refers to Christians as being "members of the household of God." One of our priesthood passages speaks of the church as "God's own people" (1 Pet. 2:9). Fred's critics were partly right in what they implied. It is not primarily *my* church or *your* church or *our* church. It is the church of God (Acts 20:28; 1 Cor. 1:2; 2 Cor. 1:1; Gal. 1:13; 1 Thess. 2:14). Divine ownership is also reflected in the relationship of the church to Christ. Paul is fond of the analogy that the church is the body of Christ, of which Christ is the head (Col. 1:18,24; Eph. 1:22-23). Jesus Himself said, " 'I will build my church'" (Matt. 16:18).

Enough of the repetition, you say. What's the point? The point is that we often miss the point! We miss it when we circumscribe the church to *our* local church or *our* denomination. We miss the point when we think in national terms. We often miss the point even when we talk about the church as a democracy. The church is a theocracy (the rule of God) and a Christocracy (the rule of Christ) before it is a democracy.

The church is the church of the living God. What does God own when He owns the church? He owns a people. We've been teaching children wrongly for years: "Here's the church, and here's the steeple. Open the door, and there are the people." Correction! "Here's the building, and here's the steeple. Open the door, and there's the church." What the latter lacks in rhyme and rhythm it makes up for in New Testament theology. Buildings are used as metaphors for the church in the New Testament (1 Cor. 3:9; 1 Pet. 2:5; Eph. 2:19-22), but buildings are never the church in the New Testament. Our ancestors were wise in referring to the building as the meeting house where the church gathered. Even then, we must remember that the church is the people, whether meeting or mobile, gathered or scattered, on Monday as well as on Sunday. Priests are priests everywhere and at all times.

The nature of God's possession, the church, is obviously obscured when *church* becomes *building* in the minds of Christians or non-Christians. Moreover, the nature of the church is confused if we think of church as an institution instead of a people. Institutional structures of some type are both necessary and inevitable if the mission of the church is to be effective. In other words, the people whom God calls must structure their lives together. The problem comes when Christians value institutional concerns, such as programs and property, more than the people. Institutions are made for the *ekklesia*, not the *ekklesia* for the institutions.

Institutionalism perverts the meaning of church. As I said at the outset of this chapter, however, individualism also distorts the meaning of biblical community. Saved as individuals, we are called to be God's people in a communal setting. It is only there that we are able to grow into the fullness of the measure of Christ.

So whose church is this? It is God's. And what does He own? A people. And they are flawed! The church is divinely owned but humanly sinful. Here is another miracle of grace that we resist maybe even more than God's mercy for our individual lives. God's *ekklesia* is human and therefore sinful. Too often we live with what Dietrich Bonhoeffer called a "clamorous desire for something more" than what actually composed the church at Corinth and Philippi or what constitutes the church at Macon or Birmingham or Corsicana. Composing all those churches are sinners saved by a gracious and forgiving God.

I have often said to my students that the doctrine of total depravity is necessary to understand rightly the church. "Just as surely as God desires to lead us to a knowledge of genuine Christian fellowship," Bonhoeffer said, "so surely must we be overwhelmed by a great disillusionment with others, with Christians in general, and, if we are fortunate, with ourselves."[2] The church would have to belong to God. Given its constituency, no one else would want it! Although often we either blister the church with words of rebuke or make outlandish claims for its infallibility! God treats the church with grace, both in His calling it into existence and in His continuing support despite its sinfulness. That's why it is the church of the living God.

This is the saints' church! There were footprints on the beach before we walked on shore. Others have gone before us. The gates of hell have not prevailed against Christ's church. One way to respond to the question, Whose church is this? is to answer in terms of its historical and universal identity.

Historical! Paul wrote to the Ephesians and to us, reminding them and us that we are "fellow citizens with the saints and members of the household of God, built upon the foundation of the apostles and prophets" (Eph. 2:19-20). Of course, in its most basic sense the church is built upon our Lord Jesus. Paul, in this Ephesian passage, goes on to say of the church that Christ is "the cornerstone, in whom the whole structure is joined together" (Eph. 20:21-22). And to the Corinthians Paul said, "No other foundation can any one lay than that which is laid, which is Jesus Christ" (1 Cor. 3:11).

After making his confession at Caesarea Philippi that Jesus is "'the Christ, the Son of the living God,'" Peter was told by Jesus who Peter was. "'You are Peter, and on this rock I will build my church'" (Matt. 16:18). Jesus was not proclaiming

Peter to be a pope. Jesus was saying, however, that on folk like Peter, with all his future equivocating and unrocklike qualities, and on confessions like Peter's the church would be constructed throughout history.

You and I entered the *ekklesia* late. We stand on the shoulders of those who helped to ignite the spark and keep the fire going. Others came along and fanned the flame with confessions like Peter's and worked to see that the church would provide warmth and light throughout the years. Whose church? All those priests who preceded us in the halls of Christian history.

Roman Catholics and some others make too much of All Saints' Day and for wrong reasons. But we Baptists probably make too little of those who passed us the baton of faith. Every local Southern Baptist church is a memorial church: first to Christ, who loved us and gave Himself for us, and second to those who followed in His steps and established local churches such as yours and mine. The priesthood did not begin with us, because the *ekklesia* did not start with us.

Nor does it end with us, our local churches, or our denomination. Jesus said, "'I will build my church.'" His reference is clearly to His one people. The sublime theme of Ephesians is God's eternal purpose in establishing and completing the church of Jesus Christ that includes all the redeemed of all times.

Local churches are expressions of the church. We Baptists recognized this long before some confused the issue in the nineteenth century by claiming that the local church is the only church. Southern Baptists affirmed a view truer to the Scriptures when they revised The Baptist Faith and Message in 1963. Article VI of that confessional statement highlighted the church as "a local body of baptized believers," but it added the following sentence: "The New Testament speaks also of the church as the body of Christ which includes all of the redeemed of all the ages." We latter-day priests are surrounded with what the Book of Hebrews calls "so great a cloud of witnesses" (12:1). Those witnesses reach way back into history and all around the globe.

This is the world's church! Whose church is this? If you answer the question in terms of ownership, the church belongs to God. If you answer the question in terms of its historical and universal identity, this is the saints' church. But if you answer the question in terms of mission and purpose, the church belongs to the world. The church's mission is in the world. There is no church apart from mission. The church is God's called-out people; but those who have been called out of the world are sent back into the world. There is a message to be proclaimed. There is a ministry to be performed.

This theme of the mission of the church, which is the responsibility of the priesthood of believers, will be developed more completely in the next chapter. Note here, however, that mission to the world has always been at the center of God's call to His people. God began creating a people for service when He called Abraham. "I will make you a great nation, and I will bless you, and make your name great, so that you will be a blessing . . . and by you all the families of the earth shall bless themselves" (Gen. 12:2-3). That was the old Israel, called to bless the world.

Likewise, through the new Israel, the church, God's manifold wisdom is to be made known (Eph. 3:10). His purpose in Christ is to "unite all things" (Eph. 1:10). We priests of the church are, like Paul, stewards of God's grace and love for the world. Our task is not simply to create mental health for the priesthood. Our buildings are not just for our use. Our prayers must be guarded for their self-centeredness, both in our personal lives and in the lives of our churches. Our giving should be monitored for its self-serving ends.

One tragedy of our churches is that they are motivated by self-interest. When we ask the question, Whose church is this? and answer it in terms of the mission of the church, other questions become easier to handle. The only budget question is, Whom does this serve? The only curriculum question is, Does it make things plainer? The only youth question is, Does this facilitate their growth as servants? The only mission question is, Does this get the word out? The only long-range planning question is, Does this put us in a position to bless somebody?[3] The church, in a fundamental way, belongs to the world.

This is our church! Fred's critics were mostly wrong, but partially right. That *was* Fred's Baptist Church, not his by him-

66

self, but his in fellowship with all other believers who met at 200 South Trenton. It is *my* church only if I know how to say *our* church. If you answer the question, Whose church is this? in terms of daily function, the answer is clear: *the church belongs to believers operating on equal footing in a particular place.* The answer contains three affirmations, all of which are grounded in the Bible and reflected concretely in the Baptist tradition.

Affirmation 1: the church is local. No need to debate this point, not if you have a Bible in your hands. "To the church of God which is at Corinth" (1 Cor. 1:2); "to all God's beloved in Rome" (Rom. 1:7); "to the church of the Thessalonians" (1 Thess. 1:1); "Aquila and Prisca, together with the church in their house" (1 Cor. 16:19); "to Nympha and the church in her house" (Col. 4:15)—the list is almost endless, and the point is obvious. The church is local. It is not invisible. It is seen in flesh and blood at 511 High Place or 2100 Monument Boulevard or whatever your local church's address is.

Is it a contradiction to say that the church is both universal and local? Are we blowing hot and cold air from our mouths at the same time? No! Such a dual emphasis is the clear teaching of the New Testament, because there is only *one* body of Christ, *one* people of God, *one ekklesia.* But there are many expressions of that one church. In the words of Frank Stagg, "It may contradict logic but not fact to say that there is but one church, yet it is found at many places at one time."[4]

Affirmation 2: the church is a local body of believers. The New Testament has not a thread of evidence that the church was composed of any people but those who had made voluntary commitments to Christ as Lord. The church did not consist of believers and unbelievers. The church consisted of "saints," those who had chosen to respond to God's call and who had been set apart for His service. Every Christian is a saint, and only saints comprise the church. So manifest is this conclusion for New Testament Christianity that the issue is never raised in the first century. Only later, with the emergence of infant baptism, was the issue focused.

When Baptists came along in the seventeenth century, they made the idea of a believers' church one of their cardinal emphases. Baptists contended that to demand a regenerate church, made up of believers only, was the only way to declare the biblical nature of the church. Therefore, they emphasized a "gathered" church rather than a "parish" church. A gathered church was made up of people who voluntarily united in Christian fellowship. One had to decide to join the gathered church. Entrance was through conversion by conviction. Not so with the parish church. One could be a member of a parish church by virtue of involuntary baptism as an infant.

Affirmation 3: the church is a local body of believers who carry out their work on equal footing with one another. This same truth can be stated in terms of the doctrine of the priesthood of believers. Only priests compose the church, and there is no hierarchy in the priesthood. This is what E. Y. Mullins described as "the ecclesiastical axiom: all believers have a right to equal privileges in the church."[5]

The popular evangelical Anglican John Stott has written a compelling book on the laity called *One People.* While he does not emphasize the term *the priesthood of believers,* he explains the meaning of the term masterfully. And he hammers home, again and again, the idea of equality in the church. This equality, says Stott, is based on God's "calling of the whole Church, and of every member of the Church, without any distinction or partiality."[6]

He points to our focal passage, Ephesians 2—3, and Paul's use of four Greek compounds—"fellow citizens," "fellow heirs," "fellow members," and "fellow partakers" (Eph. 2:19; 3:6)—to enforce the "undifferentiated common participation of all God's people in all the blessings of the gospel." Stott recognizes, as we shall in chapter 6 of this book, a diversity of function among the members. Diversity of function for Baptists, however, is never inequality of standing. All Baptists need to hear and heed John Stott, the Anglican: "I do not hesitate to say that to interpret the Church in terms of a privileged clerical caste or hierarchical structure is to destroy the New Testament doctrine of the Church."[7] Consider what is implied in answering "Whose church is this?" with "A local body of believers with equal privileges."

PERSONAL LEARNING ACTIVITY 6

Read each statement below concerning the church. If you feel that the statement is true, circle *T* for true. If you disagree with the statement, circle *F* for false.

T   F   1. A person can worship and serve God on his own as well as within the fellowship of the church.

T   F   2. Watching and listening to Christian television and radio programs is an acceptable substitute for being involved in a local church.

T   F   3. It is more accurate to speak of the church as God's church than to speak of it as the people's church.

T   F   4. Buildings are not the church. Buildings are meeting places where the church gathers.

T   F   5. The main concerns of a local church should relate to people and mission rather than property, programs, and institutions.

T   F   6. The Baptist Faith and Message refers to the church as a "local body of baptized believers."

T   F   7. The Baptist Faith and Message also refers to the church as the body of Christ "which includes the redeemed of all the ages."

T   F   8. A church is made up of people who have made voluntary commitments to Jesus Christ as Lord.

The Priesthood of Believers Within the Local Church

Again, let us be sure that we understand what is meant when we say that a local body of believers with equal privileges is *our* church. The local church is not a private club. It is not *ours* in that kind of possessive sense. But in another sense—in the sense of duty and responsibility and stewardship of discerning God's will—this *is* our church. *Our* church, not *my* church. The pronoun is plural, not singular. It speaks of community, not individualism; togetherness, not personal property.

Once a pastor was called rather suddenly to visit a man

who had suffered his first heart attack. The patient had been placed in an oxygen tent to ease the stress on his heart. Understandably, he was frightened by the tent and all that it suggested. At an appropriate moment, the pastor zipped down the side of the oxygen tent, put his head inside, and spoke calmly to his friend, "Now that we are both inside this thing, let's breathe this air together."

That is the spirit of a local Baptist church. *Our* tent is our particular local fellowship. We breathe the air of life and grace and accountability together, without any outside interference or internal domination by any individual. There is equality among the priesthood in a local Baptist church because it is a believers' church. And that means that the church government is believers' participation, the Bible is the believers' book, the Lord's Supper and baptism are believers' ordinances, and worship is believers' praise.

Church government is believers' participation. Generally speaking, there are three basic types of church government. They are episcopal, presbyterian, and congregational. In episcopal church government, authority is placed in the hands of one person, usually a bishop. In presbyterian church government, authority is vested in a small group, often called elders, within the local church. In congregational church government, authority is placed in the hands of all the members of the church. Baptists have always been and should always remain congregational in church order.

Honesty compels us to acknowledge that the New Testament does not describe in detail how the church should be structured. Proof texts from various parts of the New Testament may be called on to support all three types I have mentioned. If, however, you affirm the basic principles inherent within the priesthood of believers—equal access to God's grace for all, equal standing before God, and equal responsibility to God—you are driven to congregationalism as the most biblically appropriate way for a local church to function.

In congregational church life *every* believer has an equal voice and a single vote. That is why a local Baptist church describes itself as a democracy. It is not within the power of any individual, including the pastor, to determine God's will for the congregation. Authority to decide who will teach, who will serve as deacons, who will be ordained as ministers, who will serve as pastor, who should be disciplined and how, and anything else affecting the life of the local church is decided exclusively by the congregation in a democratic church business meeting. If these matters are not decided by *all* the members of the church in conference, the church is not functioning in a Baptist way.

Congregational church government is always subject to being undermined. Probably the most perennial threat to congregationalism is the passivity of the believers themselves. The privilege of functioning as a community of equals is abdicated when members do not assume responsibility for church life. One of the most conspicuous examples of this is the relative unimportance that many church members attach to the church business meeting.

The church business meeting is not an afterthought or an unimportant postscript in the life of the church. It is a strategic meeting of the congregation in which the privileges of the priesthood of believers are to be exercised. To ask with an edge in your voice, "What are *they* doing down at that church?" is more of a self-indictment than anything else. It reflects a lack of involvement in the policy-making activities of the church. You are a priest with an equal voice in the church! If you fail to show up or fail to speak up when church decisions are made, you have defaulted on your priesthood. It is inconceivable that a local Baptist church would fail to have regular business meetings through which church life is guided by all the priests. If, however, you are a member of such a church, you should seek to persuade your church to return to the Baptist way of congregational decision making.

Congregational church government is often threatened by the passivity of the priesthood itself, but it is also endangered by the activity of authoritarians. A few summers ago I spoke to a meeting of the associational directors of missions from across the Southern Baptist Convention. I asked them, "What is the major issue you face in the churches of your association?" Expecting them to identify some of the currently debated theological issues, I was shocked by their response. The issue they identified was pastoral authoritarianism.

71

What forces have created such an unbaptistic idea? I believe that one is the influence on Southern Baptists of concepts emerging from portions of the charismatic movement and ministries that emphasize a "chain of command." Both of these, in varying degrees and in various ways, have popularized the hierarchial principle, which Baptists have long resisted. A hierarchy, whether in Roman Catholicism or Protestantism, destroys the doctrine of the priesthood of believers.

Second, I believe that some Southern Baptists have been enormously impressed with the size and growth of independent, non-Southern Baptist churches. In my opinion, some of these so-called independent Baptist churches are more episcopal than congregational in church government. The pastors of some of these churches *dictate* to the church rather than serve with the church. Consequently, the priesthood of believers and congregational church government are either minimized or totally destroyed. Of course, power groups in the church or elected leaders who try to impose their authority on the church are also damaging to the life of the church. 1 Peter 5:2-3 admonishes church leaders to "tend the flock of God that is your charge, not by constraint but willingly, not for shameful gain but eagerly, not as domineering over those in your charge but being examples to the flock." If we are to have more shared congregational leadership in our churches, both members and clergy must recover the cardinal Baptist principle of the priesthood of believers.

PERSONAL LEARNING ACTIVITY 7
Church business meetings are one way that Baptist people express their belief in congregational government of the local church. What are some of the strengths and weaknesses of the business meeting in your church?

_____

_____

_____

What are some things that would make the business meeting in your church more effective?

_____

_____

_____

The Bible is the believers' book. The Bible is the Word of God, and it is not restricted for reading, study, or interpretation to a select few in the church. During the Middle Ages the Bible was kept in the hands of church authorities and away from ordinary believers. The first English translation of the entire Bible, produced by John Wycliffe in the late fourteenth century, was condemned, and copies were burned. In 1525 William Tyndale completed a translation of the New Testament from Greek. Not only was this translation suppressed, but Tyndale was also put to death. The first English Bible to be officially sanctioned was translated by Miles Coverdale in 1535. From Wycliffe to Coverdale the Bible in the language of the people was suppressed by the church because it was not considered appropriate for individual Christians to read and interpret the Bible for themselves.

Freedom of access to the Bible was denied for years. And even after individual Christians gained freedom of access to the Bible, they were denied the freedom to *interpret* the Bible. Martin Luther revolted against such an idea and courageously wrote Pope Leo X, "They err who ascribe to you alone the right of interpreting Scripture."[8] An early Anabaptist, Balthasar Hübmaier, articulated even more clearly the meaning of the priesthood of believers for biblical interpretation. "Since every Christian believes for himself and is baptized for himself," he said, "everyone must see and judge by the Scriptures whether he is being properly nourished by his pastor."[9]

From their beginning in the seventeenth century, Baptists have enthusiastically affirmed the authority of Scripture for faith and practice. Baptists have insisted that this entails the privilege of private interpretation of Scripture. Baptists have no formal or informal teaching office that hands down correct interpretations. The Bible is open to all believers. If the Scriptures are to guide the lives of believers, believers must be free to follow the leadership of the Holy Spirit within the context of the local church.

The authority of Scripture for faith and practice means that Baptists are an anticreedal people. Baptists have resisted the imposition of creeds on the lives of believers. No one creed or statement of faith can summarize biblical theology. Baptists have feared creeds because of the tendency to make the creed the norm and then to coerce compliance. For Baptists, the Bible, not any human document, is the ultimate guide, and that guide is open to all believers.

The believer's right to interpret the Bible carries with it the responsibility to study and seek to understand the Bible. The right of personal judgment does not mean that Sunday School classes should sit around asking one another, "What does this mean in light of your experience?" The application of biblical truth to human experience is essential in good biblical interpretation. But other questions must be answered first. What did this mean in its original setting? When was it written? Under what circumstances? What thought patterns dominated the world of the writer? The individual believer ought to know something about the history within the Bible, the history of the Bible, and principles for interpreting the Bible. Too many of us Christian priests want the privileges without the responsibilities. We often end up permitting others to interpret the Bible for us. We forfeit both the privilege and the responsibility to those who would impose their interpretations on us.

Baptism and the Lord's Supper are believers' ordinances. Baptists have generally recognized two New Testament ordinances, baptism and the Lord's Supper. We call these *ordinances* because we believe that they were ordained by Christ Himself (Matt. 28:19-20; 1 Cor. 11:24-25). Both are for believers only, and Baptists have generally affirmed that any believer, authorized by the local church, is capable of administering the ordinances.

Historically, Baptists' first and primary concern in baptism focused on the question "Whom shall we baptize?" Our ancestors answered that question by saying, "We shall baptize only those who can make voluntary and self-directed commitments to Christ." Believers' baptism is the Baptist way of protecting the concept of a believers' church. This meant, of course, that there would be no infant baptism. It did not mean that Baptists were against infants! It meant that Baptists were *for* infants, wanting them to have the privilege and the responsibility of choosing Christ for themselves when they are old enough to understand what is involved. In a profound sense, every baptismal pool in a Baptist church is a symbol of religious liberty and of the priesthood of every believer.

From "Whom shall we baptize?" Baptists moved to the question "How shall we baptize?" The answer, of course, was immersion. Immersion symbolizes the death, burial, and resurrection of the believer with Christ, and so it is the gospel in drama. Powerful drama! The mode of baptism is important if we are to symbolize the gospel message, but so is the subject of baptism if we are to portray the true nature of the church and the voluntary dimension of faith.

The Lord's Supper portrays the high cost of believers' redemption. It is a picture of God's love for us, our communion with Him, and our communion with other believers. It is administered for believers by believers, all of whom have equal access to the Supper. The clergy has no monopoly on this ordinance. Often overlooked is some significant symbolism in the manner Baptists administer the Lord's Supper. The clergy do not serve the people. The people serve the people as they extend the bread and cup to the believer sitting next to them. The people, usually through the deacons, even serve the clergy. There is no hierarchy here! The symbolism suggests the priesthood of all believers. Each priest receives from a priest. Each priest serves a priest.

Worship is believers' praise. The New Testament, as we have previously seen, often places worship within the context of the priestly service of believers (Heb. 13:15-16; 1 Pet. 2:5). Public worship is not a spectator's sport. It is an act of the believing community. Unlike some groups, Baptists don't go to church to take communion. And we should not go simply to attend preaching. If we understood worship as the entire priesthood at praise, we would not weigh the preacher down with the responsibility of the worship hour. Too much of our corporate worship is evaluated only in terms of the brilliance of the sermon, the work of one of the priests.

The truths inherent in the doctrine of the priesthood of believers need to be incorporated into the worshiping life of the community. That calls for extensive congregational participation. The use of congregational calls to worship, congregational prayers, especially the Lord's Prayer, congregational responsive readings, congregational quotations of Scripture, and congregational singing are ways to accomplish the participation of the entire priesthood. The word *amen* is not simply a convenient way to conclude a prayer. It means *so be it* and provides an opportunity for the whole congregation to affirm what has been prayed. *Amen* is a congregational word.

A renewal of the vitality of worship, both public and private, is one of the greatest needs of our day. It will not come to corporate worship apart from the involvement of the entire community of believers. When worship services are thought of as a performance, the active community of praise changes into a passive priesthood.

PERSONAL LEARNING ACTIVITY 8
Baptists have historically resisted the imposition of creeds on the life of the believer. Why do you think Baptists have been a noncreedal people?

Notes

1. Richard John Neuhaus, *Freedom for Ministry* (San Francisco: Harper & Row, 1979), 100. Used by permission.
2. Dietrich Bonhoeffer, *Life Together* (New York: Harper & Row, 1954), 26-27. Used by permission.
3. Carlyle Marney, *Priests to Each Other* (Valley Forge: The Judson Press, 1974), 15. Used by permission of Judson Press.
4. Frank Stagg, *New Testament Theology* (Nashville: Broadman Press, 1962), 184.
5. E. Y. Mullins, *The Axioms of Religion* (Philadelphia: The Judson Press, 1908), 127.
6. John Stott, *One People* (Old Tappan, New Jersey: Fleming H. Revell Company, 1982), 24.
7. Ibid., 24-26.
8. Martin Luther, *Three Treatises* (Philadelphia: Fortress Press, 1960), 275. Used by permission.
9. William L. Lumpkin, *Baptist Confessions of Faith,* rev. ed. (Valley Forge: The Judson Press, 1969), 21. Used by permission of Judson Press.

Chapter 5
The Priesthood of Believers and the Christian Life

The doctrine of the priesthood of believers influences many major doctrines of the Christian faith. For salvation, the informing word from the priesthood of believers is *accessibility.* The emphasis is on uncoerced personal access to God's grace for personal sin. Here, the individual cannot be denied. For the doctrine of the church, the informing word from the priesthood of believers is *equality.* The emphasis is on equal privileges for all believers in the local church. Here, the community cannot be ignored. For the Christian life, the informing word from the priesthood of believers is *responsibility.* The emphasis is on ministry to the "least of these" for whom Christ lived, died, and rose again. Here, the world cannot be forsaken. The Christian responsibility to minister to the world is what E. Y. Mullins described as "The Social Axiom: Love Your Neighbor as Yourself."[1]

A casual reading of the Bible, both Old and New Testaments, makes it plain that faith is no private possession to hoard. Either the gospel drives us outside ourselves, or else it has not claimed our inner selves. We are not catch basins but conduits of God's care and concern. It is not enough for the prodigal to come down the road to the Father's house shouting, "I'm back! I'm back!" or "I'm saved! I'm saved!" There are cows to be milked, fields to be plowed, and crops to be harvested! God is interested in more than our personal salvation. Too many of us priests of God and of Christ are preoccupied with the dynamics of guilt and grace and not enough with obedience and service.

The important pronouns are not *I* and *my* and *mine,* but *we* and *our* and *ours.* Nothing illustrates this emphasis more pointedly than the prayer Jesus taught us to pray (Matt. 6:9-13). Remember that Jesus taught us *how* to pray. It does not begin "My Father," but "Our Father." No leader of public prayer has the right to address God as though He is a personal possession and thereby exclude the rest of us. Jesus, morever, did not instruct us to ask to be lost in isolated communion with God. He urged us to pray that the Kingdom would come on *all* the earth. And it is not *my* but *our* daily bread, not *my* but *our* trespasses, not deliver *me* but *us* from evil.

As the title indicates, this chapter concerns the Christian life. The emphasis, however, is on the Christian life in the community of the church and for the community outside the church. Solitaire Christianity is a perversion of the faith. The sign of Christ in the world is the body of Christ, the people of God, the *ekklesia.*

The Christian life, therefore, must be understood within the boundaries of the church, the church gathered and the church scattered. God calls the church into existence. He also sends the church on mission. Praying to God for the disciples and for us, Jesus said, "'As thou didst send me into the world, so I have sent them into the world'" (John 17:18).

"As thou didst send me . . . "! There is our model. What was He sent to do? How did He go about doing it? Where did He do it? Incarnation is the key. God in Christ is the clue. "Christ in you" is the continuation. "So I have sent them . . . "! A priesthood not wrapped in its own piety but in the pain of the world—there is the sending!

What does it mean to be sent as Jesus was sent? What do we do? How? Where? First of all, the mission is descriptive, not prescriptive. Local priesthoods are on the same general mission, but specifics of the task change from congregation to congregation.

Ernest T. Campbell, former pastor of the Riverside Church in New York City and one of the genuinely superb preachers of our time, spoke of a diner on the corner of 11th Avenue and 43rd Street in New York City that he frequently visited. For good food, the rule of the highway is to eat where the truckers eat. The rule of the city, says Campbell, is to eat where the cabbies eat. At this particular diner, cabs are always in the parking lot.

One night as Campbell lined up to pay his bill, he was preceded by a cab driver. After the cabbie paid his bill, he asked the cashier for ten dollars worth of change in quarters! As he braced for a confrontation, Campbell thought, "Of all the nerve, asking for ten dollars in quarters!" Most restaurants don't even like for you to pay with a big bill, much less to ask to change one in quarters.

But there was no confrontation, no harsh frowns or words. Calmly reaching into the drawer beneath the cash register, the cashier presented the cabbie with a role of quarters. No mystery exists here! Cabbies need change. The diner that wants to serve cabbies will have change available. Campbell then asks: "Should all food establishments have such change available? No. Should this diner have such change available? Yes." All restaurants serve food but not to the same people or at the same price. Unity of purpose exists among all God's priesthoods active throughout the world. There is not, however, uniformity of procedure or sameness of strategy. Every church does not do mission exactly alike; however, every church is on mission.

One way to focus the question of how the priesthood of believers affects the Christian life is to ask yet another question: How are we to love our neighbor and our local community and our world? For the members of each local church in the Southern Baptist Convention to answer that question thoughtfully and prayerfully would issue in a burst of redemptive creativity like we have never known. Answering in a general way, I suggest we look at the priesthoods to which we belong as sacrificial servants, glad heralds, sympathetic confessors, and courageous prophets.

PERSONAL LEARNING ACTIVITY 9
Read John 17:18. What do you think it means to be sent into the world as Jesus was sent into the world?

The Priesthood as Sacrificial Servants
The nature of the Christ-calling is unmistakable. It is hard and we resist, but it is clear—clear because His own mission was clear. He came to be expendable! Jesus knew what it meant to be Messiah. It meant one *anointed* to be *suffering servant*. The Confuser could come to Him alone in the wilderness (Matt. 4:1-11) or in the public words of Peter at Caesarea Philippi (Matt. 16:22-23), but the response was the same: "Get behind me, Satan!" He would not be confused about the

shape of His calling. His was the way of obedience through sacrificial service. He did not come to drive Rome into the sea and be exalted as military hero. He did not come to establish a political party and rule with an iron fist. He was no power-driven religionist dominated by ambition cloaked in pious greed.

Christ is lamb, not lion (John 1:36). Ask Him the absurd, "Who is the greatest in the kingdom of heaven?" and He clarifies kingdom values and embarrasses your values by placing a child in your midst and lecturing on humility (Matt. 18:1-4). Put your mother up to asking Him for you and your younger brother a place of prominence and power in His kingdom, and He says, " 'Whoever would be great among you must be your servant'" (Matt. 20:26). And He adds, "even as the Son of man came not to be served but to serve, and to give his life as a ransom for many" (Matt. 20:28).

Christ the Lamb confuses our lionlike values. The first are last, and the last are first (Matt. 19:30). The exalted are humbled, and the humbled are exalted (Matt. 23:11-12). Mary sang it (Luke 1:47-55), Paul described it (Phil. 2:3-7), but Christ lived and died it. And His disciples—then and now—do not understand it! Or maybe we understand too well and resist it. Maybe we resist the responsibility of priesthood just as we resist the mercy of priesthood.

To be sure, those early disciples could not fathom the meaning of the Messiah as sacrificial servant. Following Peter's majestic confession at Caesarea Philippi, Jesus, in the latter part of His ministry, spoke three times of His coming sacrifice at Jerusalem. These passion predictions are found in Mark 8:31; 9:31; and 10:33. T. W. Manson correctly points out that each of these sayings "is accompanied by a contrasting piece displaying the selfish ambition, pride, and prejudice of the followers of Jesus."[2] At the first saying Peter rebuked both Christ and the idea of sacrificial servant (Mark 8:32). In the second episode Jesus' prediction of suffering is followed by the disciples' argument over who among them was the greatest (Mark 9:33-35). And following the third prediction, James and John came forth with their pleas for personal priority (Mark 10:35-38).

Apparently, no one had heard a word He said! No wonder!

On the heel of describing His crucifixion, Jesus had called for their crucifixion. After spelling out what kind of Messiah He was to be, He described what kind of followers they were to be: "'If any man would come after me, let him deny himself and take up his cross and follow me. For whoever would save his life will lose it; and whoever loses his life for my sake and the gospel's will save it'" (Mark 8:34-36). There is the nature of our priesthood. Self-denial! Self-crucifixion! Life losing! Just like the Lamb, we arrogant lions are to be sacrificial servants. Do we still want to be priests?

Chester Quarles, a twentieth-century Mississippi saint, did not think so. Speaking to a group of us evolving preacher-boys one night twenty-five years ago, he blasted, "Too many ministers have a guest complex; we are not guests; we are hosts." We are not called to be served; we are called to serve—sacrificially! But that is a word for the entire priesthood. It is a word for your priesting and mine.

One of the most famous passages in the New Testament is Philippians 2:1-11. Written not in a palace, but in a prison, these are words peculiarly relevant for our priesthood. Some of these verses describe what it means to have the "mind" of Jesus. Paul admonishes:

Have this mind among yourselves, which is yours in Christ Jesus, who, though he was in the form of God, did not count equality with God a thing to be grasped, but emptied himself, taking the form of a servant, being born in the likeness of men. And being found in human form he humbled himself and became obedient unto death, even death on a cross (Phil. 2:5-8).

This is no simple lesson in humility. Paul is pointing to the Jesus way of self-giving. The utter self-sacrifice that characterized the mind of Christ Jesus is what the Philippians needed in the midst of their petty squabbles.

Halfway through writing this book, I discovered another book on the general theme of priesthood. The authors tell about interviewing Eberhard Bethge, the friend and biographer of Dietrich Bonhoeffer, who died as a martyr under Hitler. Asked what he thought Bonhoeffer would be saying to the church today, Bethge responded: "'At the end Bonhoeffer saw in his experience . . . that the church, with its dominating stature in the Western world, must now step down below.'"[3]

"He . . . emptied himself, taking the form of a servant." "The church . . . must now step down below." But we cannot take that long step to servanthood as long as we ask, "How much does it cost?" rather than, "How much can we give?" We cannot take that step by designing church programs that market religion to "attract the attractive"[4] rather than the six groups Jesus identified with. You remember those: the "hungry," the "thirsty," the "stranger," the "naked," the "sick," the ones "in prison" (Matt. 25:34-46). How much of your church budget touches those six groups? How many of your church programs are constructed with those persons in mind? Out of all the human hours invested in your church's ministry, how many hours do the six groups get?

Whatever priesthood meant in Israel's earlier days, by the time of the first century it was associated with offering sacrifices to God. When first-century Christians appropriated the term *priesthood* and applied it to themselves, they also assumed the priestly function of offering sacrifices. But for Christians, the sacrifices were not those of dead animals. The Christian sacrifices were living and consisted of their very lives (Rom. 12:1). Priesthood is an awesome responsibility. It is to make ourselves expendable for those whom Jesus identified as "the least of these."

The Priesthood as Glad Heralds
Hendrik Kraemer in *A Theology of the Laity* made much of our last point, that Christian priesthood is sacrificial service to the world in the name of Christ. In fact, he said:

> Being Church-centred, regarding the world of the Church as the safe refuge from the world, is a betrayal of its nature and calling. Only by not being or not wanting to be an end in itself, the Church arrives at being the Church.[5]

Kraemer insisted that "the church *is* mission." The very essence of the church is to come down on the side of the hurting and the hurt in the world.

A derivative of the church's mission, however, is missions. Priests must serve sacrificially. Priests must also speak. There are wounds to bind, mouths to feed, naked to clothe, and prisons to visit. There is also a word to speak. We are to be sacrificial servants. We are also to be glad heralds of the word we have heard. As priests, said Peter, we are to "declare the wonderful deeds of him who called you [us] out of darkness into his marvelous light" (1 Pet. 2:9).

Speaking is just as hard for some as serving is for some others. The priesthood has been engaged in a needless and fruitless dispute for years over speaking and serving. An observation: those who speak easily often serve reluctantly; those who serve easily often speak reluctantly. Enough judgment lies in that for each of us to silence all caustic accusations. If I resist either serving or speaking, it probably points to a need in my own life.

Jesus served. Jesus spoke. "From that time Jesus began to preach, saying, 'Repent, for the kingdom of heaven is at hand'" (Matt. 4:17). Was He browbeating? Brainwashing? Indoctrinating? Manipulating? No, He was seeking to help people find purpose and direction for their lives. Jesus came to talk with us about God. He talked about God without the slightest trace of intimidation. He was not intimidated, and He would not intimidate. In the natural flow of Jesus' life He talked about God to strangely diverse people in various ways and in different places. In fact, He seldom missed an opportunity to relate life as He encountered it to God as He knew Him. His spoken call for repentance was a plea for reconciliation between people and the true Source of their lives.

Look what He did with that word of reconciliation. He left it to us to speak as He had spoken. "You shall be my witnesses" (Acts 1:8). He "gave us the ministry of reconciliation" and entrusted us with "the message of reconciliation." "So," Paul adds, "we are ambassadors for Christ, God making his appeal through us" (2 Cor. 5:20).

Why are we so tongue-tied and timid with this message? Why do we not, in the natural flow of our lives, do what Christ did? Have we let the worst in some evangelism deter us

85

altogether from legitimate priestly work? Yes! Do we believe there is a need for reconciliation? Yes! Do we believe that the word entrusted to us is the answer? Yes! Do we impose too much on ourselves as moral prerequisites to verbal witnessing? Yes! Nobody is "good enough" to speak this marvelous word! If we waited until we were "good enough," the world would never know of Christ.

But how do you speak? How do you untie your tongue? To begin with, notice how many times within the course of a week you are witnessed to personally about something. Within a matter of four days four different persons witnessed to me about four different subjects. First, my barber, upon discovering that I was trying to lose weight by walking, became unrestrained about a fitness center that he uses a few blocks from my house. Second, a church member who knows some of my tastes accosted me after a meeting one evening and enthusiastically told me about a popular radio program, "A Prairie Home Companion," featuring Garrison Keillor. He wanted me to share his joy. Third, a preacher-friend witnessed to me about the excellence of Fred Craddock's preaching. Fourth, a Christian friend, a recovered alcoholic, spoke movingly to me of the power of Alcoholics Anonymous in his life.

Here are six lessons I learned from those "evangelists." One, each of them knew that I had some interest in their message, and they took advantage of an opening to speak with me. The lesson for priests: look for openings. Two, the "witness sessions" occurred in natural ways during the routine events of the day. The lesson for priests: we would never need church visitation programs if priestly work were done in the natural flow of life, but we would need more church buildings to house the people. Three, not one of the four persons spoke down to me because of what I did not know or did not have. The lesson for priests: how you say what you say may be as important as what you say.

Four, although they had different shades of enthusiasm, all four had something they genuinely wanted me to try, hear, or appreciate. They were glad heralds. The lesson for priests: talk about a part of the gospel that excites you and is relevant for the listener. Five, each of the four either gave me something, brought me something, or offered to bring me something following the conversation. My barber delivered to my doorstep a brochure on the fitness center; the church member offered to get me a videotape of Keillor on TV; my preacher-friend brought me several tapes of Craddock's preaching; the AA advocate gave me a copy of the Serenity Prayer, which is used by that organization. The lesson for priests: show your interest by what you do, as well as what you say. Six, the fact that none of the four were experts in their respective subjects did not keep them from speaking their joy. The lesson for priests: you don't have to be "the chief priest" to be a glad herald.

Was their speaking effective? I was almost persuaded but turned back before joining the fitness center. I have read one of Keillor's books and have listened to his show occasionally, but basically, I'm lukewarm. I now think Fred Craddock is one of the three best preachers in the United States. My sensitivity to alcoholics is heightened, and my appreciation for AA is deepened. I am convinced, however, that the four were not thinking primarily of results. They spoke because they had something they sincerely wanted to say that they thought I really needed to hear. Everybody witnesses to something! Christian priests are glad heralds of Him who called them into the bright light of God's love and Christian community out of the dreary darkness of sin and alienation. As in worship so in witness, the priesthood is not passive audience but active participant.

The Priesthood as Sympathetic Confessors
In Hebrews 5 the writer describes two major characteristics of the Jewish high priest. The priest is divinely appointed, but he is also sympathetic with human weaknesses. The writer put it this way:

> *Every high priest chosen from among men is appointed to act on behalf of men in relation to God, to offer gifts and sacrifices for sins. He can deal gently with the ignorant and wayward, since he himself is beset with weakness. Because of this he is bound to offer sacrifice for his own sins as well as for those of the people (Heb. 5:1-3).*

It is a fact that you and I are Christian priests divinely appointed. But can we identify? Can we "deal gently with the ignorant and wayward"?

Our model for that is not simply the Jewish high priests; it is the Great High Priest, Jesus, the Son of God. "We have not a high priest who is unable to sympathize with our weaknesses, but one who in every respect has been tempted as we are, yet without sin" (Heb. 4:15). Good priesting, we said in chapter 2, is impossible without identification. We have to identify with the guilt laden and the morally bankrupt, those whom Hebrews calls "the ignorant and wayward."

We priests of God and of Christ are to be sympathetic confessors. A confessor is one who hears a confession. Many people struggle under the burden of a guilty conscience. That's why whoever brings acceptance brings healing. And whoever cannot accept acceptance cannot be healed. And whoever refuses to share the inmost self precludes healing. So what does James say to the priesthood? "Therefore confess your sins to one another, and pray for one another, that you may be healed" (Jas. 5:16).

Note the mutuality in the text: "Confess your sins to one another." Confessor is also confessee. That is the only way identification occurs. Shepherds are also sheep. Priests do not reach down; they reach across! Condescension is not the posture of the priest. Our ability to "deal gently" is rooted in the self-awareness that we ourselves are "beset with weakness." Hunter and Johnson said it well in a brilliant chapter describing the local priesthood as "A Place of Pastoral Care."

> *Pastoral care practiced as a community is characterized by mutuality. It is not a matter of the strong stooping to help the weak, the clear-headed advising the muddled, or the healthy and sound superior condescending to the groping and broken inferior; it is a journey taken together in which there is the possibility of our being pastors and priests to each other.* [6]

Priests serve sacrificially. They speak gladly. They also listen sympathetically and confess willingly. Listening and confessing, James said, are linked to our healing. There is no healing in hiding, only despair and self-recrimination. The priesthood as sympathetic confessors constitutes a community of the forgiven who are forgivers. But there can be no forgiveness or healing without repentance. "Renewal comes to the church not through programs, techniques, fads, pep rallies, and gimmicks, but through *metanoia*—repentance in response to the good news of the gospel."[7] *Metanoia*, the road to healing, will not happen apart from gentle confessors who identify with the repenting one.

Priesting through serving as sympathetic confessor is not rooted in ordination. One is not certified for this task by virtue of office. Certification is by identification. One can be trained to become a better confessor, a task to which the church should commit itself, but the essential prerequisites are a knowledge of one's own sinfulness and an experience with God's grace. Redemptive listening in the priesthood cannot be relegated to pastoral counselors, theologically trained clergy, or specialists in the church of any kind. Again, there are not enough "professionals" to meet the dimensions of the pain. More importantly, however, one purpose of the priesthood is to serve as a community of sympathetic confessors.

The priestly community exists to extend community. Community is extended through serving and speaking, but it is also extended as the priesthood constructs an atmosphere of acceptance, of confession and healing, and of repentance and forgiveness. This task is as difficult as, if not more difficult than, serving sacrificially and speaking gladly, because it speaks to our accessibility to others' pain and our vulnerability in exposing our own. Both hurt. Neither will occur where there is no priesthood of pain sharers. Pretending we have no pain will guarantee that others will not confess theirs. Acting as though there is no healing is a betrayal of the gospel and of our priesthood.

An example of the priesthood as sympathetic confessors is the Sunday School class to which I belong. Periodically, the class interrupts its routine study to hear a fellow priest tell his or her own story and how it intersects with God's story. This is no exercise in "You let me see through you, and I'll let you see through me." This is not spiritual stripteasism. The members are interested not in group therapy but in the gospel of hearing and healing, confessing and accepting, and wall-shattering and community-extending. Everything is not told, nor should it be! But enough is said to draw us closer as pilgrims and priests.

What have I learned from these priests and their stories? First, some of the best priesting comes from unexpected sources. Priests without diplomas and degrees and pedigrees are often the ones who most "deal gently with the ignorant and wayward." Second, what hurts the most to tell facilitates community the best and brings healing the quickest. Third, the need for believers to get to know one another goes beyond Friday night socials and Saturday cookouts. Those events are often hiding places, not a community of priests. Fourth, the capability of the priesthood to share pain and to celebrate joy is real, and it is rooted in the gospel.

The Priesthood as Courageous Prophets
The prophethood of all believers is closely related to the priesthood of all believers. In fact, the two cannot be separated, but we work hard at the task. For if we can divide, we can evade. Being prophetic is a troublesome task. By prophetic I do not mean predicting the unknown future; I mean confronting the unjust present. In this area the priesthood calls for "the preacher" or somebody else "to do it for us"— unless, of course, *our* unjust present is in need of rebuke, and in that case we do not want to hear about it at all. Few *want* to be prophets, and those who ache for the assignment usually do not deserve a hearing.

Note the way we divide the roles of priest and prophet to evade the latter and identify with the former. "He is a priestly person!" That means he is personal, understanding, unperturbable, noncontroversial, and nonconfrontive. He visits a number of nursing homes and is called on to do a lot of funerals, weddings, and counseling. Priests of this type spend their lives tranquilizing already tranquil waters. Who doesn't prefer that?

"He is a prophetic person!" That means he is issue oriented, unpurchasable, impossible to silence, somewhat abrasive, and a troublemaker. He perceives justice as a part of mercy, understands conflict as a means of loving, and if a pastor, is usually looking for a church! People of that ilk we appreciate only from afar, preferably from twenty-five to thirty years following their funerals!

Priesthood involves prophethood. Confessors frequently must become confronters to expedite healing. Heralds speak bad news so that good news will have a chance. Servants embrace the neglected and thereby draw the ire of the respected. The division between prophet and priest cannot be made, because it is fundamentally false, because every believer is thrown into conflicting loyalties, and because prophethood is swallowed up in priesthood.

Which was Jesus: prophet or priest? "Both," answers the writer of Hebrews (1:1-3), "and at the same time," but not in those words. In His personal encounters and with society at large, Jesus exercised both roles simultaneously. With the woman at the well, Jesus confronted her sordid past, but He also provided her the water of life (John 4:7-26). With the woman caught in adultery, He did not minimize her sin, but He did forgive her (John 8:1-11). He affirmed and rebuked Peter (Matt. 16:13-23). In the Temple, He "overturned the tables" on some, but He healed "the blind and the lame" (Matt. 21:12-14). While exposing Jerusalem's rejection of its prophets, He nonetheless yearned for its well-being (Luke 13:34). He rode in on a colt in humility, but He did ride in for the confrontation (Mark 11:4-11)!

The prophethood of believers is engulfed in the priesthood of believers. Henri Nouwen has written often and persuasively of this dual and indivisive role of the believer. While the believer must create an atmosphere of hospitality for all people, says Nouwen, hospitality has two sides to it. One side is genuine receptivity. The other side is honest confrontation.[8] Again, he says, there are two ways to guide people: inspiring and confronting. Confrontation is a form of guidance, because "a prophetic ministry which guides toward a new future requires the hard, painful unmasking of our illusions. . . ."[9] And in a book titled *Compassion,* Nouwen repeats himself for our benefit: "Compassion does not exclude confrontation. On the contrary, confrontation is an integral part of compassion. Confrontation can indeed be an authentic expression of compassion."[10]

What does this mean for the priesthood of believers? Within the priesthood it says that we have a responsibility for other priests. I may not be killed by your kindness, but I can be stunted by it when it masquerades under withheld candor. Although it is a delicate ministry, we can cultivate the ministry of redemptive criticism. Surely we must be gentle and sympathetic, but we must not be apathetic with a brother or sister, these copriests of ours. Perhaps some of our refusal to confront is not the sign of love but the absence of it. We say: "That is a personal matter." "We must not interfere." "It is none of my business." But we really mean: "I am afraid." "I may be rejected." "He may never speak to me again." When your family is in trouble, don't you take initiative and risk misunderstanding in order to be a healer? This is no call for lambasting. It is a call to help those who can be helped before it is too late. "Better is open rebuke than hidden love. Faithful are the wounds of a friend; profuse are the kisses of an enemy" (Prov. 27:5-6).

And as the priesthood faces outward toward society at large, the prophethood of believers comes into play. Injustice must be exposed and exploitation challenged. Can we serve the poor without standing up for the poor and speaking on behalf of the poor? Can we genuinely be concerned with whom Jesus called "the least of these" without confronting the social structures that help inflict the harm? Can we withdraw from the world into various forms of individual piety without challenging the reigning values of contemporary culture?

A few years back my wife went to her twentieth high-school reunion. An award was given to the class member who had changed the least in those twenty years. Although that may be an honor at a class reunion, it is an indictment in Christian living.

How long have you been a member of the Christian priesthood now? Five, ten, twenty years? Thirty, forty, fifty years? Face the questions of priestly accountability. Have you become more sacrificial in service in the name of Christ, or have you become increasingly spiritually self-centered? Have you become a more willing herald of what God did in Christ, or have you retreated into a shell of silence? Have you become more accepting and thereby extended community, or have you drawn harder and more rigid lines and thwarted community building? Have you become more willing to confront injustice in the name of Christ, or has your early idealism degenerated into a hopeless cynicism? We priests are hosts, not guests; servants, not lords; spokespersons, not silent ones; confronters, not evaders. Priesthood is freighted with responsibility.

PERSONAL LEARNING ACTIVITY 10

Every Christian is a priest. In the left column list the things you are now doing in your Christian life to serve as a priest of Jesus Christ. In the right column list some of the things you need to do to serve more effectively as a priest of Jesus Christ.

Ways I am expressing my Christian priesthood	Things I need to do to be a more effective priest

Notes

1. E. Y. Mullins, *The Axioms of Religion* (Philadelphia: The Judson Press, 1908), 201.

2. T. W. Manson, *Ministry and Priesthood: Christ's and Ours* (Richmond: John Knox Press, n.d.), 27.

3. Victor L. Hunter and Phillip Johnson, *The Human Church in the Presence of Christ* (Macon, GA: Mercer University Press, 1985), 141.

4. Ibid., 142.

5. Hendrik Kraemer, *A Theology of the Laity* (Philadelphia: The Westminster Press, 1958), 130.

6. Hunter and Johnson, 56.

7. Hunter and Johnson, 74.

8. Henri J. M. Nouwen, *Reaching Out* (Garden City, New York: Doubleday & Company, Inc., 1975), 69.

9. Excerpt from page 63 of THE LIVING REMINDER by Henri J.M. Nouwen. Copyright © 1977 by The Seabury Press, Inc.

10. Donald P. McNeill, Douglas A. Morrison, and Henri J. M. Nouwen, *Compassion* (Garden City, New York: Doubleday & Company, Inc., 1982), 124.

Chapter 6
The Priesthood of Believers and Spiritual Gifts

Every member of the body of Christ is called to priesthood, is gifted for priesthood, and should be trained for priesthood. A recurring emphasis in the New Testament, especially in Paul's writings, is that of spiritual gifts. The doctrine of the priesthood of believers is vitally related to spiritual gifts.

Back in the 1960s the Peace Corps advertised itself with an attractive slogan: "It takes all kinds to make a world; the Peace Corps takes all kinds." That is also true of the church of Jesus Christ: "It takes all kinds to make the church; the church takes all kinds." That is one of the major points Paul made in his teaching on spiritual gifts. In 1 Corinthians 12:4-6 Paul said, "Now there are varieties of gifts, but the same Spirit; and there are varieties of service, but the same Lord; and there are varieties of working, but it is the same God who inspires them all in every one." The lesson is clear. It takes all kinds to make the church!

But Paul goes on to say in 1 Corinthians 12:13, "By one Spirit we were all baptized into one body—Jews or Greeks, slaves or free—and all were made to drink of one Spirit." The lesson is clear. The church takes all kinds! All are baptized into one body: blacks or whites, laborers or white-collar workers, PhD's or high-school dropouts, male or female, preachers or plumbers, single or married, elderly or young. "All were made to drink of one Spirit."

In the previous chapter I said that the doctrine of the priesthood of believers influences several major doctrines of the Christian faith. The informing word for salvation is *accessibility,* for the church it is *equality,* and for the Christian life it is *responsibility.* For the concept of spiritual gifts, the informing word from the priesthood of believers is *universality.* Here, the insistence is that the ministry of the church cannot be restricted to one group within the church.

No person in America has written more extensively or persuasively about the universal priesthood of believers than Elton Trueblood. Recently, Trueblood wrote that the key to the renewal of the church rests in the concept of freshness. The enemy of the contemporary church, said Trueblood, is not unbelief, but staleness. Part of the staleness of the church is due to the belief that the ministry of the church depends on one group, the clergy. Freshness will not be restored until the church modifies the idea of professional ministry and replaces it with the New Testament concept of a universal ministry. Said Trueblood, "We shall not restore freshness unless and until we involve far more women and men in the ministry. . . ."[1]

The priesthood of believers calls for universal participation in the church's task of witnessing to Christ. So does the concept, so prominent in the New Testament, of spiritual gifts. The two concepts of spiritual gifts and the priesthood of all believers raise the question of the relationship between the laity and the clergy. In what sense are all believers priests? In what special sense are the ordained clergy priests? How are the two related? In the following pages we shall examine four aspects of the subject of spiritual gifts. These four are: (1) the universality of gifts; (2) the diversity of gifts; (3) the purpose of gifts; and (4) the development of gifts.

The Universality of Gifts
In the New Testament spiritual gifts are discussed in four separate passages. These are 1 Corinthians 12—14, Romans 12:3-8, Ephesians 4:1-18, and 1 Peter 4:7-11. To increase your understanding of the rest of this chapter, read all four passages of Scripture now.

Each of the gifts passages has its own specific context and purpose. In 1 Corinthians Paul responded to specific questions that the Corinthian Christians raised about gifts. Gifts had become a divisive issue at Corinth, so Paul urged unity within the church by pointing to love as the supreme gift. In Romans 12 Paul described the nature of the consecrated Christian life, and he exhorted the Roman Christians to utilize their gifts in Christian ministry. In Ephesians 4 Paul appealed to Christians to maintain the unity of the faith, and he demonstrated how gifts are to be used to build up the body of Christ. In 1 Peter 4:7-11, the only non-Pauline discussion of gifts in the New Testament, Christians are urged to be good stewards of their gifts "in order that in everything God may be glorified through Jesus Christ."

A careful reading of these four passages will demonstrate several differences. The purposes for writing about gifts, as I have just indicated, differ. Also, the gifts themselves differ from one list to another. However, some important similarities exist among the four gifts passages.

One similarity is that all four passages insist on the common source of gifts. Each Christian is gifted for Christian service *by God.* Acknowledging the varieties of gifts, Paul also reminds the Corinthians of the one divine origin of gifts. It is "the same Spirit," "the same Lord," and "the same God" (1 Cor. 12:4-6) who is the gift giver. All gifts "are inspired by one and the same Spirit" (1 Cor. 12:11), Paul says. In the Romans passage Paul likewise speaks of "the measure of faith which God has assigned" (Rom. 12:3) and of "the grace given to us" (Rom. 12:6).

The divine source of gifts is echoed in both Ephesians and 1 Peter. Ephesians 4:7 says that "grace was given . . . according to the measure of Christ's gift." And in 1 Peter 4:10 Christians are urged to be "good stewards of God's varied grace." Many things about spiritual gifts in the New Testament may be difficult to understand, but one thing is clear. Gifts come from God. My *gift,* whatever it is, is a gift *of God;* and I, therefore, have a stewardship issue on my back. No one else can exercise my gift for me, perform my ministry for me, or execute my task for me. It is mine to do because it is God's gift to me. Gifts are recognized by the church, but they are not assigned by the church. They certainly are not assigned by the ordained clergy. Gifts come from God.

Divine in origin, spiritual gifts are also universal in their distribution in the church. Every Christian is gifted. The usual Greek word for *gifts* is *charismata,* from which we get our word *charismatic.* The root word, *charis* or *grace,* denotes that which is freely given by God. When we say, therefore, that all Christians are gifted, we are also saying that every Christian is a charismatic. It is regrettable and erroneous, as is often done, to limit the word *charismatic* to persons with radiant personalities or specific gifts of speech.

"To each is given the manifestation of the Spirit," said Paul (1 Cor. 12:7). The Holy Spirit, Paul continued, apportions gifts "to each one individually as he wills" (1 Cor. 12:11). This emphasis on the universality of gifts is repeated implicitly in Romans 12:6 and explicitly in Ephesians 4:7 and 1 Peter

4:10. Scholars may debate, as indeed they do, whether spiritual gifts are natural talents intensified by the Holy Spirit or supernatural gifts that accompany conversion. Few would deny, however, that every Christian is endowed with a talent or ability to be used in the cause of Christ. Christian ministry cannot be restricted to religious professionals because spiritual gifts are not so confined.

A pastor described his participation in a conference so large that people were strangers to one another. Following dinner on the first evening of the conference, the participants formed a large circle around the dining hall. The leader began an introduction process by saying his name. But then, instead of the usual things one would say about vocation or place of residence, he said, "I bring to this gathering the gift of _____," and he identified a skill or talent or attribute of his personality. Each person did the same, stating his or her name and the unique gift brought to the group.

What if that scene were duplicated in every congregation of Christians in America? According to the New Testament, it could! And it could because every Christian is gifted by God. What if you and all other Christians in your church were given a sheet of paper and asked to identify your gift or ability, your special endowment, and then you were asked to sign your name? Here is what would happen. Few, if any, ministries of the church would go unfulfilled! Few, if any, needs in the community would go unmet! We would close the door on the idea of Christian discipleship as a spectator's sport! We would reclaim the doctrine of the priesthood of all believers! And we would stop relegating the ministry of Christ's church to the offices of the ordained!

The subject of spiritual gifts is important because, like the priesthood of believers, it speaks to the fundamentally lay character of the church. But at this point our language not only gives us away; it also demonstrates how far we have strayed from Jesus and the early church. "I'm just a layperson." "The committee has nothing but lay folk on it." "He's only a layman." "We must wait until we get a pastor." The problem is one of underestimating our gifts and minimizing our contribution.

We have forgotten! Forgotten that Jesus was a layman. Forgotten that the twelve with whom He began were laymen. Forgotten that the Book of Acts describes the activity of laypeople who *functioned* as ministers. Forgotten that the early church rejected the professional priesthood of Judaism for the universal priesthood of all Christians. Sacerdotalism, the idea of elevating religious professionals in religion, was no more operative in the mind of Jesus for Christian ministry than was circumcision for salvation. Yet one of the major obstacles to a clear understanding of ministry in the church continues to be the spiritual caste system separating clergy and laity.

With the universalizing of the priesthood in the early church, God provided gifts to all believers for the work of witnessing to the living Christ. Since all are priests and since all have spiritual gifts, all are responsible for witness and ministry.

The Diversity of Gifts

The source of gifts is God. The extent of His gifts is universal; each Christian is gifted. But the gifts come in different shapes, forms, and styles. Each of the four passages in the New Testament relating to gifts emphasizes the diversity of gifts that God gives to His people.

The variety of gifts is highlighted by the fact, as we said before, that the four lists of spiritual gifts are not identical. Moreover, Paul, especially, clearly teaches that gifts differ. In Romans 12:6 he says, "Having gifts that differ according to the grace given to us, let us use them." He begins the teaching on spiritual gifts in 1 Corinthians 12:4-5 by underlining the fact that "there are varieties of gifts," "varieties of service," and "varieties of working." Comparing the church to the human body, he said, "The body does not consist of one member but of many" (1 Cor. 12:14). And 1 Peter 4:10 refers to God's "varied grace."

This variety of gift giving by God is no act of divine caprice. It has purpose and design to it. The aim is *wholeness* and *completeness*. No one person can do it all; it takes all of us. Paul's use of the human body as an analogy to the body of Christ drives this point home:

Just as the body is one and has many members, and all the members of the body, though many, are one body, so it is with Christ. . . . For the body does not consist of one member but of many. . . . Now you are the body of Christ and individually members of it (1 Cor. 12:12,14,27).

Conformity in the body is actually deformity. That is the point of Paul's rhetorical questions in 1 Corinthians 12:17. "If the whole body were an eye," he asks, probably with a grin on his face, "where would be the hearing? If the whole body were an ear, where would be the sense of smell?" Imagine walking down the street and seeing a *body* walking toward you that was nothing but an ear! Or picture another *being* that was nothing but an *eye.* Science-fiction writers may conceive of such *bodies,* but you and I know that kind of uniformity as deformity.

In the church we *deform* the body of Christ when we try to *uniform* it. That was the Corinthian blunder. Some were isolating one gift and then exalting it above all others. They thought a part was the whole. They had a complete grasp on a partial gift. The result is deadly.

Conformity deforms. Diversity gives life. Some at Corinth longed not only for unity but also for uniformity, and they could not tolerate diversity. In my favorite TV commercial a fellow says, "Well, my broker is E. F. Hutton, and E. F. Hutton says. . . ." Apply it to the denomination. "Well, my denomination is the Southern Baptist Convention, and the Southern Baptist Convention says. . . ." How do you complete the sentence? The Southern Baptist Convention says many different things from diverse points of view through many gifted persons.

Apply it to your local church. However you finish the sentence, you must remember that your gift is not the whole. If I fail to remember that, I end up underestimating other gifts and services and ministries in my church. When I underestimate your gift, I more than likely will overestimate my gift. It takes all kinds to make the church!

Preaching is not the whole! Singing or Christian education is not the whole! Social justice or personal spirituality is not the whole. Counseling or personal witnessing is not the whole. Nor does God give all the gifts to one person to perform on behalf of the entire body. Diverse gifts distributed to all priests work together to create the whole. Underestimating my special gift to the cause of Christ is as dangerous as underestimating your particular gift.

The Purpose of Gifts

Some underestimate their own gift. Some underestimate others' gifts. But most all of us underemploy our gifts. So, shortly before He left His disciples, Jesus told a story about "'a man going on a journey [who] called his servants and entrusted to them his property; to one he gave five talents, to another two, to another one, to each according to his ability'" (Matt. 25:14-15). The five-talent fellow went out, took some risks with what had been given him, and doubled his master's money. The second man did likewise. Both were commended as "good and faithful" servants.

"'He who had received the one talent,'" Jesus said, "'went and dug in the ground and hid his master's money.'" Why not? It was a sure way of securing it. It would not be lost that way. Besides, he knew his master was a "hard man," and he did not want to go before his master empty-handed. His defense for doing nothing with what had been entrusted to him was, "'I was afraid, and I went and hid your talent in the ground.'" We may feel that he deserves sympathy, especially if we are afraid to run risks.

But sympathy he did not get. He was called a "wicked and slothful servant." My dictionary gives three synonyms for *slothful*. They are: *sluggish, lazy,* and *indolent*. Think of it! *Wicked* means *lazy* in this passage. But the master in the story was not content to reprimand the servant. He took the talent from him and gave it to the ten-talent one.

What's the point? The point is that what God puts in our hands is to be used in life. There is more to life than to travel passively through it. God's gifts are not to be buried in the ground. They are to be employed in the Kingdom.

I have always wished that Jesus had given us the ages of those three fellows in the story. My guess is that the first one was about twenty-one, a recent graduate of college and on his first job. He had no concept of a dollar. Everything he had, his parents had given to him. He would risk anything! His parents probably stayed awake at night worrying over the way he recklessly invested money in far-out schemes. And wouldn't you know it? He doubled his money!

The second fellow was about thirty-five, dressed in a business suit, studied *The Wall Street Journal,* and was facing college tuition in a few years for his two children. He, too, ran some risks, made some smart trades, and came out a winner. But this third fellow—this cautious character with the one talent—I know exactly how old he was. He was fifty. That's my age. And fifty is old enough to know that the bumps and bruises of life instill extraordinary caution. The temptation is to stay in the shallow water, close to the shore. If you run few risks, you reduce your losses! Failure is impossible when inaction is the pattern. Or is it?

Why this digression on the ages of the three servants? Because, generally speaking, the longer we live, the more inclined we are to underlive. The digression is relevant because we have an increasing number of the elderly in our churches with enormous gifts, and the temptation of age is to lie back, lie low, minimize gifts, and even bury God's gifts before it is burial time.

Did you notice that I protected myself in the above paragraph? I said that *generally speaking,* the longer we live, the more inclined we are to underlive. The exceptions are as notable as they are inspiring. Johnny Jones, a former elementary-school principal, became our director of Sunday School at age seventy. Howard Bivens became chairman of our deacons at age eighty-three. What gifts! And what courage! Not intimidated by the fear of failure, these priests of God refused to bury their gifts. Priests don't live under the threat of mandatory retirement!

However, they do live with a danger of having their gifts overlooked. While some may fail to use their gifts for a lack of courage, others do so for a lack of opportunity. Ageism, like sexism and racism, is sinful in the church not only because it is blatant discrimination, but also because it represents an enormous waste. God's gifts should not be allowed to lie dormant.

But for what purpose are our gifts? Look again at the Scripture passages that speak of gifts. A clear pattern emerges. "To each is given the manifestation of the Spirit for the common good" (1 Cor. 12:7). God has created the human body, Paul said, so that even the weaker parts of the body are indispensable. This results in unity in the body. Likewise, spiritual gifts are for the unity, not the uniformity, of the church. The members of the body of Christ are to exercise their gifts to "care for one another" (1 Cor. 12:25). Gifts are to be utilized "so that the church may be edified" (1 Cor. 14:5). "Strive to excel in building up the church" (1 Cor. 14:12), Paul admonished those at Corinth who were speaking in tongues. "As each has received a gift, employ it for one another" directs 1 Peter 4:10. And our gifts are used for the purpose "that in everything God may be glorified through Jesus Christ" (1 Peter 4:11).

Again, we may have difficulty knowing the exact nature of some of the New Testament gifts, but we should have little difficulty understanding the purpose of gifts. Our gifts are to connect with the life of the priestly community. The Bible simply will not let us off with a personal relationship to God. Discipleship goes beyond personal ecstasy, personal forgiveness, personal salvation, or personal gifts. Authentic Christian piety expresses itself in the middle of community. The real test of any gift is found in a simple answer to a simple question: Does it connect with and contribute to community? To be sure, I must not bury my gift. Neither must I view it as a personal possession for personal enjoyment. We are priests to one another, and our gifts are "for the common good."

PERSONAL LEARNING ACTIVITY 11
Read 1 Corinthians 12:4-11. According to this passage,

where do spiritual gifts come from? _____

Who gives them? _____

To whom are spiritual gifts given (vv. 7,11)? _____

For what purpose are spiritual gifts given (v. 7)? _____

_____

The Development of Gifts

If diverse gifts are universally distributed by God for the purpose of enriching the ministry of the total community, what is the role of the ordained clergy within the church? Do we even need the professional ministry of the church? Another way to pose the question is to ask if the universal priesthood of believers negates the priesthood of the clergy. The answer, of course, is that both are needed.

Before considering the relationship between the laity and the clergy, we need to emphasize a couple of points. First, the ministry of the church of Jesus Christ belongs to all believers. That is the precise meaning of the universal priesthood of believers. The universality of Christian ministry is also underscored by the New Testament emphasis on spiritual gifts. Trueblood is right. Freshness and vitality will not be restored to the church apart from the rediscovery and implementation of the concept of universal ministry. The responsibility of the church's witness to Christ is a shared ministry.

When the work of the Christian community is not a shared ministry, two tragedies occur. First, the laity is overlooked. Second, the clergy is overworked. When the laity is overlooked, the church deprives itself of God-given gifts. When the clergy is overworked, God-given gifts, which are intended to be a vital part of the whole, are distorted and transformed into the whole. In both instances the result is disastrous for the ministry of the church.

A second point needing emphasis, therefore, is that the ministry of the clergy is one function among many functions in the church. The gift of the ordained ministry is one gift among many gifts. The clergy function as priests alongside all the other priests. It is not a function *above* or *below* other ministries; it is a function *alongside* other ministries.

What, then, is the work of the clergy if it is not the exclusive responsibility of doing the ministry of the church? It is to *facilitate* the ministry of the church. In other words the ordained ministers of the church are responsible to help others in the church perform their ministry. "The pastor," says Findley B. Edge, "is to help those who are believers to grow and develop toward maturity and to equip them in their ministry of fulfilling God's mission in the world."[2]

To *facilitate* the total ministry of the church is a very different function than to *do* the total ministry of the church. A deacon was praying at a Sunday morning worship service shortly after a new pastor had arrived at the church. Well intentioned, he prayed, "Lord, bless our new pastor and help us to assist him in any way we can." But, you see, the pastor is not there to be assisted; the pastor is there to assist. Pastors are not there to perform the total ministry of the church. Pastors are there to facilitate the total ministry of the church.

In a sermon C. Welton Gaddy recounted S. E. Morrison's ironic description of a discussion that occurred surrounding the Constitution of the United States in 1787. Benjamin Franklin proposed that a session of the Constitutional Convention be opened with prayer. The delegates, most of whom believed in prayer, rejected the proposal because they had no money to pay a chaplain! That mind-set, which perceives the work of ministry to be restricted to the clergy, is a burden to a church. It contends that the only job of the laity is to pay to have the ministry performed by some other gifted priest. Such an idea is more than wrong. It is heresy.

Contrast that view of the pastor's task and the church's ministry with Ephesians 4:11-12. In the King James Version you will find the following translation:

> *He gave some, apostles; and some, prophets; and some, evangelists; and some, pastors and teachers; for the perfecting of the saints, for the work of the ministry, for the edifying of the body of Christ. (KJV)*

The passage reads as though there are three tasks of the pastor. These are to: (1) perfect the saints; (2) do the work of the ministry; and (3) edify the body of Christ. If this translation is accurate, one of the purposes of the pastor is, indeed, to *do* the work of the ministry.

But there is a misplaced comma in the King James Version!

Compare the King James Version with the Revised Standard Version:

His gifts were that some should be apostles, some prophets, some evangelists, some pastors and teachers, to equip the saints for the work of ministry, for building up the body of Christ.[3]

Notice carefully that there is no comma after "to equip the saints." This is true to the original language of the Bible. The work of the pastor is not threefold but singular: "to equip the saints for the work of ministry, for building up the body of Christ." You can understand why some interpreters have referred to the comma after "saints" in the King James Version as the fatal comma.

If the task of the pastor is to do the work of the ministry, the rest of us are responsible to support him, pay him, and pray for him. However, if the task of the pastor is to equip the saints for their ministry, the entire picture of ministry changes. The pastor's role and ours, as well, have been radically transformed. The work of the pastor is to equip or furnish believers for the work of ministering with a view to building up the church.

The work of equipping the saints for the ministry by itself is big enough, broad enough, and comprehensive enough! But in football language, we nonpastor priests with our unused gifts are guilty of piling on the clergy. One person cannot carry the entire team! One gift is not the whole! One priest does not make a priesthood of believers!

In the almost twenty years of my teaching ministry, I have been privileged to serve as interim pastor of a number of Southern Baptist churches. To be honest, I am amazed and become somewhat depressed when I hear various church members in the same local fellowship describe what they want in their next pastor. I am amazed at the concept of ministry that emerges. And I am depressed for the poor pastor who is bold enough to accept the assignment.

The conversation usually begins with, "What we need in our next pastor is _____," and the list is endless. "What we need is a good pulpiteer." They need a preacher! "What we need is a good Bible educator." They need a teacher! "What we need is a good administrator." They need an executive! "What we need is someone to point the way." They need a leader! "What we need is someone to help us build this new building." They need a contractor! "What we need is a people-person." They need a personality! "What we need is a person with a social conscience." They need a prophet! "What we need is a soul-winner." They need an evangelist!

The list is not only discouraging; it is impossible. Even worse, it perverts the work of pastors and ignores the work of all the rest of us. Paul made it clear in his writings that all the gifts of the body of Christ are not incorporated into one person. The overarching calling of the pastor, as Ephesians 4:11-12 says, is to develop the gifts of others. The clergy has an equipping ministry.

But the clergy cannot equip others for ministry if they themselves are not equipped for their ministry of equipping. This speaks to two areas of theological education for pastors. One is formal theological education, that which occurs in colleges, seminaries, and Bible colleges. Southern Baptists have never required formal theological education for their pastors, but we certainly should never minimize it. To say that it is unrequired is not to say that it is unneeded. We need our schools to be the very best theological institutions they can be. And we need them to focus on developing clergy who are able to develop the gifts of the laity in local churches.

The second area of theological education is informal and often forgotten by both clergy and churches. This is *continuing* theological education. Much ministerial burnout is "rustout." Too many clergy seek to live too long on their school experiences! A formal education is not designed to tell one what one needs to know for the rest of life; it aims at teaching one how to learn what one needs to know for the remainder of ministry. Pastors must keep studying. Churches should make that possible, if not mandatory, by providing periodic study leaves for their clergy. Such study leaves are not personal rewards for the professional ministry. They are ways of ensuring that the equipping ministers stay equipped for developing the gift of the entire priesthood.

If the New Testament ideal is to be achieved of diverse gifts working together to present a unified witness for Christ, we need someone working to bring this goal to fruition. To say it another way, if the universal ministry of the priesthood is to be realized, we need some specific priests laboring at this task. That is the calling and, as Ephesians 4:11 suggests, the gift of pastors.

That pastoral gift can be exercised in many ways, but I will mention only three. First, *identify* gifts of other priests. Watch for undeveloped and unused powers, point them out, and support them in their infancy. Many Christians have found deeper significance in their discipleship because a caring pastor uttered an authentic and specific word of confidence in abilities that had gone unnoticed. Gifts cannot be developed if unidentified.

Second, *specify* needs of ministry. The more specific the expression of need, the more likely the possibility that gifts will emerge to meet those needs. In a sermon one Sunday morning a pastor lifted up the need for someone to spearhead a ministry for the poor in the community. A woman stopped the pastor after the service and said, "You identified this morning one of my concerns that matches some of my gifts; I'll do it!" A new ministry was born, and a dormant gift was activated.

Third, *motivate* through teaching/preaching. Whatever else the clergy are, they are servants of the Word of God. "When the minister of the church is no longer a servant of the Word, the laity of the church will no longer be prepared, informed, and trained as a priesthood in the world."[4] Equipping involves motivating.

In light of the New Testament teaching on spiritual gifts and the universal priesthood, our prayer should be, "Lord, bless our clergy, and help them to use their gifts to assist us in using our gifts so that together we may build up the body of Christ."

PERSONAL LEARNING ACTIVITY 12

What are your spiritual gifts? _____

_____

How do you believe your gifts can be developed? _____

_____

How do you think your gifts can be used in the ministry of

your church? _____

_____

Notes

1. Elton Trueblood, *Quarterly Yoke Letter,* 28, No. 3 (September 1986), 1.
2. Findley B. Edge, *The Doctrine of the Laity* (Nashville: Convention Press, 1985), 77.
3. *The Holy Bible,* Revised Standard Version (Nashville: Holman Bible Publishers, 1982).
4. Victor L. Hunter and Phillip Johnson, *The Human Church in the Presence of Christ* (Macon, GA: Mercer University Press, 1985), 113.

Chapter 7
The Priesthood of Believers and the State

In 1925 and again in 1963 the Southern Baptist Convention adopted a statement called The Baptist Faith and Message. The last article in that document deals with the very important subject of the relationship between church and state, and it is printed below in full. Read it slowly and carefully.

God alone is Lord of the conscience, and He has left it free from the doctrines and commandments of men which are contrary to His Word or not contained in it. Church and state should be separate. The state owes to every church protection and full freedom in the pursuit of its spiritual ends. In providing for such freedom no ecclesiastical group or denomination should be favored by the state more than others. Civil government being ordained of God, it is the duty of Christians to render loyal obedience thereto in all things not contrary to the revealed will of God. The church should not resort to the civil power to carry on its work. The gospel of Christ contemplates spiritual means alone for the pursuit of its ends. The state has no right to impose penalties for religious opinions of any kind. The state has no right to impose taxes for the support of any form of religion. A free church in a free state is the Christian ideal, and this implies the right of free and unhindered access to God on the part of all men, and the right to form and propagate opinions in the sphere of religion without interference by the civil power. [1]

Following the statement are eighteen Scripture references that provide biblical support.

Although this article in The Baptist Faith and Message is titled "Religious Liberty," it obviously includes more than a single emphasis on religious liberty. It contains a cluster of ideas, including the sovereignty of God, the separation of church and state, the obligation of state to church and of Christians to the state, the origin of government, freedom of religion, and the priesthood of believers. Without changing the content of the article, one could just as easily and accurately title it "The Priesthood of Believers and the State."

How does the doctrine of the priesthood of believers affect the Christian's relationship to the state? Does your role as a Christian priest involve your role as a citizen of government? How are citizenship and discipleship joined by the concept of the priesthood of believers? For the state, the informing word from the priesthood of believers is *liberty*. The emphasis is on the freedom of religion for all citizens of the state. Conscience cannot be repressed.

Robert Goodrich once told of a man who took his little granddaughter with him on a New York visit. They rode the ferry out to see the Statue of Liberty. The child, of course, was awed by the sight of the great arm holding up the huge torch. On the return boat to Manhattan she kept looking back at the statue. That night when she could not sleep, her grandfather asked if something was troubling her. "I keep thinking of the lady with the lamp," she said. "Don't you think somebody ought to help her hold it up?"

Since their beginning in the seventeenth century, Baptists have been committed to helping hold up liberty. Of course, that commitment emerges from Baptists' concern for liberty for themselves. But they have been concerned for liberty for others, as well. A major doctrinal foundation for the Baptist concern for liberty has been the doctrine of the priesthood of believers. In civil matters this doctrine has caused Baptists to insist upon three ideas: (1) subordination of loyalty to the state to the lordship of Christ; (2) liberty from the state for all citizens; and (3) participation in affairs of state by all believers.

Subordination of the State
The article on religious liberty in The Baptist Faith and Message begins with the words "God alone is Lord of the conscience." Christ, not Caesar, is Lord of the Christian's life and of the church. That theme is present, indeed pervasive, in both biblical and Baptist history.

Christianity entered the Roman world affirming but one sovereignty, and that was the sovereignty of the God and Father of the Lord Jesus Christ. The Christian affirmation of the sovereignty of God is rooted firmly in the Jewish heritage of the Old Testament. Summarizing the believer's duty toward God and neighbor, the Ten Commandments began with a call for the recognition of God's sovereignty. "'You shall have no other gods before me'" (Ex. 20:3), said God. Probably the most frequently repeated words in the Jewish tradition are those found in Deuteronomy 6:4-5. Known as the Shema, they speak of Israel's sole, supreme loyalty: "'Hear, O Israel: The Lord our God is one Lord; and you shall love the Lord your God with all your heart, and with all your soul, and with all your might.'"

Later, when Jesus was asked which was the first and greatest commandment, he repeated the Shema (Mark 12:29-30). For Jesus, all other loyalties were subordinated to an unqualified devotion to God. Throughout the entire New Testament the refrain "King of Kings, and Lord of Lords" echoes as it does in Handel's majestic *Messiah*. The misunderstanding of that affirmation is as dangerous to twentieth-century Christians as it was for the first-century believers. Christianity appeared to many critics of the faith in the first century as a subversive, rather than a supportive, element in the Roman Empire. That perception was a mistaken one. But there was no mistaking the fact that acceptance of Christ as Lord made all human institutions, including the state, less than absolute.

Since their beginning in the seventeenth century in England, Baptists have also insisted on subordination of loyalty to the state to the lordship of Christ over their lives. The first plea for complete religious freedom in the English language was written by Thomas Helwys. A courageous Baptist layman, Helwys led the first Baptist church on English soil. Helwys's plea for freedom was titled *A Short Declaration of the Mistery of Iniquity*. He sent a copy to King James I, and he enclosed the following handwritten dedication.

> Heare o King, and dispise not ye counsell of ye poore, and let their complaints come before thee.
> The King is a mortall man, and not God therefore hath no power over ye immortall soules of his subjects, to make lawes and ordinances for them, and to set spiritual Lords over them.
> If the King have authority to make spirituall Lords and lawes, then he is an immortall God, and not a mortall man.

O King, be not seduced by deceivers to sin so against God, whome thou oughtest to obey, nor against thy poore subjects who ought and will obey thee in all things with body life and goods, or else let their lives be taken from ye earth.

God Save ye King

Tho: Helwys.[2]

"The King is a mortall man, and not God!" There is the Baptist emphasis on God's sovereignty! Helwys was not advocating anarchy or subversion. On the contrary, he was arguing for good Christian citizenship. He was affirming the priority of discipleship over citizenship and of the "King of Kings" over the king of England.

How does the theological emphasis of the sovereignty of God and of the priority of Christ over Caesar compare with specific New Testament teachings about the Christian's relationship to the state? At least three models of the believer's relationship to the state may be identified in the New Testament. If taken in isolation from one another, they may appear to be contradictory. If interpreted together, however, they are mutually supportive and clarify the Christian's ultimate loyalty.

The first model of the believer's relationship to the state is found in Matthew 22:15-22. In this episode some Pharisees and Herodians sought to trap Jesus by forcing Him to choose between the religious loyalty to Jewish sectarianism and the civil loyalty to the Roman Empire. Lathering Jesus with flattery, they began by saying, " 'Teacher, we know that you are true, and teach the way of God truthfully, and care for no man; for you do not regard the position of men' " (Matt. 22:16). Then came the trap: " 'Is it lawful to pay taxes to Caesar, or not?' " (Matt. 22:17).

The heart of Jesus' response is found in verse 21: " 'Render therefore to Caesar the things that are Caesar's, and to God the things that are God's.' " In this succinct sentence Jesus pointed to both the legitimacy and the limitations of the state. Both Caesar and God constitute loyalties, but there is no question about which is the ultimate allegiance.

In Romans 13 Paul provides a second model of the believer's relationship to the state. Here Paul accentuates the legitimacy of the state, stressing that the state is divinely ordained. "Let every person be subject to the governing authorities," Paul says. And he continues, "For there is no authority except from God, and those that exist have been instituted by God" (Rom. 13:1).

Paul viewed the Roman Empire under which he lived as an appointed servant of God; the state deserved the respect and obedience of the believer. It must be remembered, however, that at the time of Paul's writing Rome tolerated diverse religions, including Christianity. Paul's words certainly should not be interpreted as applying to all situations, especially oppressive and idolatrous governments. His salutary emphasis in this passage is a reminder that our freedom in Christ does not exempt us from the laws of the state. Discipleship does not negate citizenship.

The third model of the believer's relationship to the state is found in Revelation 13. The circumstances are quite different here from those in which Paul penned Romans 13. Rome's policy of toleration had been transformed into persecution. Many believe that this passage has its setting in a time when emperor worship had been revived, and Rome sought to impose this "religion" upon its citizens, including the Christians. Whereas for Paul in Romans 13 the state was an appointed servant of God, many feel that John saw the Roman Empire as the "beast rising out of the sea."

Rather than admonishing Christians to submit to the Roman government, John encouraged them to persevere in spite of it. The totalitarian claims of Rome were to be rejected even though martyrdom would be the consequence. John emphasized the limitations of the state over the lives of believers.

When these three models are interpreted together, a couple of important principles for believers emerge. First, the state is a recognized and legitimate authority. As shall be discussed later in this chapter, this means, among other things, that Christians can and should justifiably participate in matters of state. But although the state is a legitimate authority for Christians, the lordship of Christ over the church also means that Christianity is not dependent for its survival on any special form of government. Indeed, the Christian church has often thrived under the most unfavorable of governments.

Inherent in the doctrine of the priesthood of believers are some basic democratic concepts. Unquestionably, this doctrine finds its fullest expression of freedom where democratic governments exist, such as in America. But the Bible does not point to one particular form of the state as the Christian ideal. The state is a legitimate authority, but certain forms of the state are not necessary for the church. The security of the church is found not in the state but in the Lord.

A second important principle is that the authority of the state is limited for Christians by the ultimate loyalty that is due God alone. Christians are priests of God and of Christ. They are not priests of the state. Nationalism, in whatever country, cannot be made into "God." This leads not only to poor citizenship for Christians but also to heretical discipleship. "God alone is Lord of the conscience." For the believer, the state is always subordinate to the lordship of Christ.

Liberty from the State

Just as the priesthood of believers asserts the priority of the lordship of Christ over the state for believers, it also affirms the state's role to preserve religious liberty for the individual conscience. The doctrine of the priesthood of believers cries out for freedom of religious expression. Thoroughly democratic in character, the priesthood of believers is characterized by equality and freedom. These dual emphases of equality and freedom carry over into the civil realm in demanding religious liberty for all citizens of the state. In the words of The Baptist Faith and Message, "The state owes to every church protection and full freedom in the pursuit of its spiritual ends."

What are the foundations for religious liberty? On what do Baptists rest their case that individuals should be free to believe without coercion, practice their faith without constraint, and spread their faith without hindrance? Religious freedom may be based on the ancient idea of human reason and the need for a society of equals to concede to one another the right of free discussion. But this has not been the primary appeal of Baptists.

Baptists have anchored their passion for religious liberty in certain theological affirmations. The equality and freedom inherent in the priesthood of believers evolve from spiritual convictions that have to do with (1) the nature of God; (2) the nature of humans; and (3) the nature of faith.

Religious freedom is a fundamental freedom that is rooted in the very nature of God. According to Genesis, a sovereign God dared to create us as free beings. Throughout the Old Testament God is portrayed as a liberating God. Under divine command, Moses issued the word to Pharaoh "Let my people go!" God set Himself against persons and institutions that restricted the freedom of His people. And the entire thrust of Jesus' life and ministry was to free people from all that would keep them from fulfilling their destiny under God.

Freedom runs much deeper, therefore, than constitutional right or governmental gift. God is the source of liberty, not nations or courts or human law. No person can commit any more flagrant act of arrogance than to assume that he can give another human being liberty. That is what Peter and John were saying to their adversaries who wanted to silence the word about Jesus: " 'Whether it is right in the sight of God to listen to you rather than to God, you must judge; for we cannot but speak of what we have seen and heard' " (Acts 4:19-20). Peter and John could be locked up, but they could not be shut up! Their liberty to speak their faith was rooted in their freedom under God. That was precisely the same argument used by our Baptist ancestors in colonial America when religious liberties were curtailed. Liberty cannot be given by any other person or institution because it is only God's to give.

Religious liberty is also based on the biblical view of persons. Created in the image of God, a human being is the crowning work of God's hands. The dignity and worth of every individual are theological concepts based on biblical revelation. When the psalmist reflected on the majesty of God, he asked, "What is man that thou art mindful of him?" (Ps. 8:4). Answering his own question, he affirmed, "Yet thou hast made him little less than God, and dost crown him with glory and honor. Thou hast given him dominion over the works of thy hands; thou hast put all things under his feet" (Ps. 8:5-6). Persons are not mere things, not toys for politicians to play with, not robots for religious leaders to command. Human personality is sacred and is life's highest value. To deny any person the freedom necessary to follow the dictates of conscience is to debase God's creation.

Religious liberty is founded on the nature of God and the biblical view of people, but it is also established on the nature of biblical faith. I discussed the voluntary nature of faith in chapter 3. You may want to review that section at this time. To be genuine, faith must be free. Authentic faith cannot be coerced or denied by the state. The priesthood of believers argues that faith must be chosen, not imposed. A voluntary response to God is necessary if discipleship is to be vital and genuine. Anything less than a voluntary response only produces a hypocritical faith.

Contending that the individual conscience must be free from civil interference in religious matters, the Baptist passion for religious liberty runs in several directions. Among other things, this means freedom *of* religion, freedom *from* religion, and freedom *for* religion.

Freedom *of* religion! Why? Because every individual has the right to direct access to God! Because Caesar is limited, and God has not given the state any power to compel in matters of faith! Because "equal rights to all and special privileges to none is the true ideal."[3] Because the Bible says that every person is accountable to God and to God alone! The Baptist emphasis on individual soul competency declares that the civil government is incompetent to tell people what to believe, how to believe, and how to express that belief in worship. These are not issues to be "rendered unto Caesar." Those are freedoms that Caesar should guarantee and preserve.

In pleading for religious liberty, Baptists have not been begging for mere religious toleration. They distinguish between religious liberty and religious toleration. No one has made this point any better than George Truett. Speaking of Baptists, Truett said:

Their contention is not for mere toleration, but for absolute liberty. There is a wide difference between toleration and liberty. Toleration implies that somebody falsely claims the right to tolerate. Toleration is a concession, while liberty is a right. Toleration is a matter of expediency; while liberty is a matter of principle. Toleration is a gift from man, while liberty is a gift from God. It is, therefore, the consistent, insistent and persistent contention of our Baptist people, always and everywhere, that religion must be forever voluntary and uncoerced, and that it is not the prerogative of any power, whether civil or ecclesiastical, to compel men to conform to any religious creed or form of worship, or to pay taxes for the support of a religious organization to which they do not belong, and in whose creed they do not believe. God desires free worshippers, and no others.[4]

Baptists have wanted, and they should continue to want, absolute liberty!

And what they want for themselves, they should advocate for *all* people. Our insistence on freedom *of* religion, therefore, must include freedom *from* religion. The right not to believe is as sacred as one's right to believe. Baptists contend for the principle of religious liberty "not only for themselves," said Truett, "but as well, for all others—for Protestants of all denominations, for Romanists, for Jews, for Quakers, for Turks, for Pagans, for all men everywhere."[5]

Baptists also stand for freedom *for* religion. This is the freedom to evangelize and persuade. Religious freedom is far more than the right to worship according to conscience. It is the freedom to share one's faith with others, to teach and preach without reprisal. It is the freedom to seek to convince in an open marketplace of ideas. For the government to fail to protect that freedom for any person is to permit abridgment of one's civil rights. Evangelistic freedom is crucial for Baptists because they do not replenish themselves through births but through rebirths. Again, however, what Baptists ask for themselves—the right to propagate their point of view—they must also ask for all people of all faiths, as well as for those without faith.

The Baptist appeal for civil protection of religious liberty expresses itself politically in the concept of separation of church and state. Four patterns of church-state relations are discernible in Christian history and in the modern world. The first is that of the church *above* the state. This was present through much of the medieval era, when one form of faith, Roman Catholicism, dominated in both civil and religious domains. Inevitably, the power of the state was used to buttress the claims and to extend the influence of this one group. Religious harassment and persecution resulted; minorities were denied freedom of expression because religious pluralism was viewed as a threat to the "true" church. Even in nations where the political reality of church *over* state does not exist, the mind-set of wanting one form of faith to dominate may be present. In America, for example, Christians must be careful in calling on the state to support our religious views with the power of government. If not, we will find ourselves functioning *de facto* as did Roman Catholics in the medieval era.

The second pattern of church-state relations is that of the church *under* the state. This pattern existed in France during the French Revolution and is evident today in the Soviet Union. In this instance the power of the state is used to deny religious freedom. The state, not a specific church or faith, becomes totalitarian in its claims. The state, in fact, becomes a "faith," subjugating all other faiths to its authority. In this instance freedom of expression is denied because pluralism is perceived as a threat to the government.

A third pattern of church-state relations is an alliance between a particular church and the state. The most prominent example of this exists in England, where the Anglican Church is the established church but where freedom of religious expression is granted to other groups. This same pattern was present in colonial America. Not until the early nineteenth century was this approach finally abolished in America. And Baptists were front and center in calling for the disestablishment of government-supported churches. Government is not to discriminate on the basis of the religious sentiments of its citizenry, but rather to provide equal standing before the law for all.

The fourth form of church-state relationship is the separation of church and state. This has been expressed as the church and state *side by side.* This is what The Baptist Faith and Message intends when it says, "A free church in a free state is the Christian ideal." It is a ringing affirmation of "liberty and justice for all" and of the principle that diversity of opinion need not be feared. Baptists have historically not only embraced this approach, through Roger Williams and others, but also pioneered this pattern. It is the only approach, they believe, that provides maximum religious freedom for the entire citizenry.

Participation in the State

From the outset of this book I have emphasized that the doctrine of the priesthood of believers carries within it the dual emphasis of freedom and responsibility. And just as the priesthood of believers argues for liberty from the state for all citizens, it also urges participation in the affairs of state for all believers. C. Welton Gaddy made this point in his book *Profile of a Christian Citizen:*

> *The people of God, though ultimately accountable only to God, are expected to be responsible in their relations to government. The New Testament is quite specific on this point. Codified laws of the state are to be obeyed so that order may be maintained and justice facilitated (Rom. 13:5; 1 Pet. 2:13-16; Titus 3:1). Taxes are to be paid faithfully in order that government may be adequately supported (Rom. 13:6-7; Matt. 22:21). Prayers are to be offered on behalf of the nation as a whole as well as specifically for those in leadership positions (1 Tim. 2:1-3).*[6]

The doctrine of the priesthood of believers, however, suggests that responsibility for society goes beyond obeying laws, paying taxes, praying for officials, or voting one's convictions in the polling booth. Just as the doctrine of the priesthood of believers universalized the priesthood in terms of race and sex, it also universalized the priesthood in terms of vocation of calling and location of ministry.

The universalizing of the priesthood in terms of vocation of calling means that believers who are politicians are just as much priests of God as are believers who are preachers. Once a bright and committed Christian collegian who was struggling with his life's vocation came to see me. "I am torn," he said, "between going into politics and becoming a pastor." He wanted to know which calling I thought he should pursue. Of course, I could not tell him what God's will was for his life. I could and did remind him, however, that the fundamental calling is to be a devoted disciple of Jesus Christ. "You will be a minister of Jesus Christ," I encouraged him, "whether you end up in the pulpit or in City Hall."

Gordon Strachan, a former White House assistant, was engulfed in the infamous Watergate scandal of the Nixon administration. Undergoing interrogation by the Senate Select Committee, Strachan was asked the following question by Senator Joseph Montoya: "Now because of Watergate, many young people are . . . saying that public service is not as attractive as before Watergate. . . . What advice do you have for these young people?" Strachan responded succinctly, "Stay away."

That must never become the counsel for Christians! The political arena is too important for the destiny and character of a nation for Christians to back up and back off. The work of the priesthood is no longer restricted to the temple. To absent themselves from the power centers of society is for Christians to abdicate their priestly calling. " 'The temple has always been downtown,' "7 said Carlyle Marney. And *downtown* means the Chamber of Commerce, the school board, the city council, and the halls of Congress.

We cannot do priestly work "downtown" by pronouncing government as inherently evil and withdrawing into monastic isolation. But neither can we do good priestly work "downtown" by ignoring the pluralism of American life and trying to transform the state into the church. To participate actively in government does not mean that we should expect the state to promote the gospel or to pressure others to abide by our views. The principle of free expression in the American heritage is something for which Christians, especially Baptists, should stand up and cheer! In that regard, the American heritage corresponds to the Baptist heritage, especially the doctrine of the priesthood of all believers. It is the duty of every Christian to let his or her voice be heard in civic concerns. It is also the responsibility of every Christian to guard for others the freedom of conscience treasured for oneself. The separation of church and state has never meant the disengagement of church people from the affairs of government. Participation in the affairs of the state, however, certainly has never meant an attempt to restore the medieval pattern of church over state.

So what impact does the doctrine of the priesthood of believers have on the Christian's relation to the state? The priesthood affirms only one sovereign Lord, operates within the context of freedom, and urges participation in matters of government. For the state, the key word from the priesthood of believers is *liberty*. All citizens should have freedom of religious expression. The priesthood of believers shouts that conscience cannot be repressed.

PERSONAL LEARNING ACTIVITY 13

Read Matthew 22:21. In this verse Jesus said, " 'Render therefore to Caesar the things that are Caesar's, and to God the things that are God's.' " For a Christian living in today's world, what does it mean to " 'render therefore to Caesar the things

that are Caesar's' "? _____

_____

_____

What does it mean to render " 'to God the things that are

God's' "? _____

_____

_____

_____

Notes

1. *The Baptist Faith and Message,* statement adopted by the Southern Baptist Convention, May 9, 1963, 19.

2. Sydnor L. Stealey, ed. and comp., *A Baptist Treasury* (New York: Thomas Y. Crowell Company, 1958), 12-13.

3. E. Y. Mullins, "The Baptist Conception of Religious Liberty," in Walter B. Shurden, ed., *The Life of Baptists in the Life of the World* (Nashville: Broadman Press, 1985), 59.

4. George W. Truett, "The Baptist Message and Mission for the World Today," in Shurden, 115-116.

5. Ibid., 115.

6. C. Welton Gaddy, *Profile of a Christian Citizen* (Nashville: Broadman Press, 1974), 12.

7. Carlyle Marney, *Priests to Each Other* (Valley Forge: The Judson Press, 1974), 13. Used by permission of Judson Press.

Chapter 8
Your Priesthood and Your World

Had I discovered it in time, I might have begun this book with the following quotation. Since I didn't, I would like to begin this last chapter with it.

> *If you were asked, Are you . . .*
> —*a believer? You would probably answer, "Of course, I have faith."*
> —*a disciple? You would surely say, "Yes, I follow the way of Christ."*
> —*a minister? You would probably be a bit more hesitant, but you would probably say, "Yes, I attempt to serve others."*
> —*a priest? Would you say, "Why, no, not really. They had priests long ago in Israel, but not today except in certain churches, and they are supposed to be different, aren't they?"*[1]

The thrust of this book may be summarized in a single sentence: *You are a priest who belongs to a priesthood.* But why do so many Baptists find it difficult to apply the title of *priest* to themselves? As indicated in chapter 1, maybe it is because the word is so unbaptistic sounding, so Roman Catholic sounding. Or maybe it is because we have forgotten our own Baptist heritage, which is so dominated by the phrase *the priesthood of believers.* Or maybe a false modesty says that we are not good enough to be called *priests.* Maybe we do not want the awesome freedom or the staggering responsibility of priesthood. Or could it be that we have not read the Bible often enough or carefully enough? How could we miss it in Exodus 19:6; 1 Peter 2:5; 2:9; Revelation 1:5-6; 5:9-10; and 20:6? Not only the concepts but also the very words *priests* and *priesthood* are found in the Bible. We are "priests of God and of Christ" (Rev. 20:6), and we are "a holy priesthood" (1 Pet. 2:5).

Perhaps no single idea would renew our individual discipleship or revitalize our churches like the rediscovery and reaffirmation of the doctrine of the priesthood of believers. Indeed, I believe Christian history demonstrates that when this idea languishes and lies dormant, personal Christianity deteriorates, church life declines, and the world suffers for lack of an authentic witness to Jesus Christ. When the idea reasserts itself, however, I believe a new power and passion invade individual lives, churches, and a needy world.

The fact that *you are a priest who belongs to a priesthood* is nothing less than spiritual fire! But that fire can be snuffed out by the forces of history. That fire can blaze out of control and blow in wrong directions. And tragically, that fire can fail to be utilized. In this last chapter, therefore, we shall examine three aspects of the doctrine of the priesthood of believers. One is the possible historical erosion of the idea. The second is the possible doctrinal distortion of the idea. And the third is the needful implementation of the idea in our world.

The Erosion of the Priesthood of Believers
In our kind of world your role as priest is always under threat of extinction. History demonstrates that the idea of a *universal* priesthood of believers is constantly under attack by the concept of a *restricted* priesthood. Inclusive priesthoods are forever in danger of becoming exclusive priesthoods. The biblical concept of ministry as belonging to *all* the people of the church is easily perverted, ignored, or both. What results is an idea of ministry relegated to an elite clergy. Usually, this pattern of erosion occurs so gradually that it goes unnoticed.

In discussing the biblical and historical foundations of the priesthood of believers in chapters 1 and 2, I made allusions to this tragic transformation from a universal to an elite priesthood. While occurring many times in history, this pattern of change can be witnessed at three pivotal points in biblical and Christian history. These are in Jewish history, in early Christianity, and in the Protestant Reformation.

Look first at Jewish history. Against the background of a divided humanity as reflected in the Tower of Babel experience, Abraham is called to a universal task of reconciliation (Gen. 12:1-3). For certain, the call to mission is to Abraham and to his descendants. The task, however, is to bless "all the families of the earth" and to enlist them in the mission of reconciliation. The reconciled were to become reconcilers. The blessed were to become blessings.

Subsequently, under Moses Israel was given a covenant from God. Basic to that covenant was the proposition that the whole of Israel was to become a "kingdom of priests and a holy nation" (Ex. 19:6). All were called to be priests in God's world. And even though God permitted and ordained the development of a special order of priests through the tribe of Levi, He never intended for the priesthood of the people to be obscured by the priesthood of the Levites. But by the time of Jesus of Nazareth, a cleavage had emerged between the people and the priesthood. Distinction of function in priesthood had become separation of the people from priesthood. Participation in ministry by all the people degenerated into observation and support of ministry by a few people. Erosion became transformation. Israel had become a kingdom of priest-watchers rather than a kingdom of priests.

Then came Jesus, the layman from the tribe of Judah (Heb. 7:14), who created the new Israel of God, the church. Priesthood was again universalized. All who followed Christ—male and female, Jew and Gentile, slave and free—became a "chosen race, a royal priesthood" (1 Pet. 2:9). Christ restored the essential oneness of the people of God. He abolished spiritual privilege.

The Book of Acts is a history of a church on fire not because of the pomp, power, and prestige of the clergy. It is a book about lay-priests who had found mercy and wanted to share it. They had been ordained by mercy into the one priesthood of God.

But the one priesthood did not mean similarity of function or gift (Rom. 12:3-8; 1 Cor. 12—14; Eph. 4:1-13; 1 Pet. 4:10-11). The New Testament allows distinction within the priesthood. Pastors have a necessary role to play. They are to "equip the saints for the work of ministry" (Eph. 4:12).[2] Again, however, erosion occurred. Within a short span of time, by the second century, the equippers for ministry came to be viewed as the *only* ministers. Distinction *of* ministry became separation *from* ministry. The laity became observers. What had happened to Israel had happened to the church. Priests had become priest-watchers. This pattern of separation of the people from the clergy continued until the time of the Reformation.

Then in the sixteenth century came Martin Luther, the former priest of the Roman Catholic Church, who recognized the biblical teaching that the priesthood was not limited to the clergy but included all believers. Protestantism restored the cherished New Testament doctrine of the universal priesthood. But while Luther and other Reformation leaders tried valiantly to eliminate the separation between the clergy and the laity, erosion of the priesthood of believers again occurred.

In Roman Catholicism the separation between the clergy and the laity had developed largely because of the belief that the priests were responsible for and sole guardians of the sacraments. The people at large became passive recipients of these priestly sacraments. In Protestantism, however, there was a different development. Rather than emphasizing the sacraments, Luther and his followers exalted the preaching ministry of the clergy. And rather than becoming passive recipients of the sacraments, the Protestant laity now became passive recipients of biblical truths as preached by the clergy. Tacitly and tragically, the accepted assumption was that the ministry of the church was the concern of the clergy. Distinction of function within the universal priesthood degenerated into separation of the laity from the priesthood. The laity had become listeners. The priesthood became priest-watchers.

Do you see now why I said that in our kind of world your priesthood is always under threat of extinction? History documents this fact. In Judaism, the universal priesthood became passive observers. They watched an elite priesthood offer sacrifices. In early Christianity the universal priesthood became passive recipients. They watched an elite priesthood administer the sacraments. In Protestantism the universal priesthood became passive listeners. They watched an elite priesthood deliver sermons.

Even though Baptists have a noble heritage of stressing the priesthood of believers, there is no reason to expect that they are exempt from the erosion process. What can be done to stop the erosion? How do we reverse the flow? First, we must begin at the only point of beginning for Christians. We must read the Bible again. Too often we have taken our cue for the life and work of the church from models provided by corporations and governments. These models have a chief executive officer or a chairman of the board or a prime minister at the top, with everyone else functioning in a supportive role. This model of the ministry of the church plays havoc with the biblical pattern of the priesthood of all believers. According to the Bible, we are priests who belong to a priesthood, and the only High Priest is Christ Jesus Himself (see Heb. 4:14-16).

Second, by returning to the biblical teaching, we would reaffirm that ministry belongs to the whole church. The erosion of the doctrine of the priesthood of believers cannot be thwarted as long as the *laos,* the people of God, perceive themselves as passive participants in the mission of the church. Their calling is not merely "to show up, to put up, and to shut up."[3] Christian discipleship is something a believer does, not a program one merely supports or a responsibility unloaded on the clergy. No one else can do your discipleship for you.

Third, the erosion can be halted by clarifying the role of the clergy. They are equippers, enablers, facilitators, multipliers, and playing coaches. They are ministers who help other ministers minister (see Eph. 4:11-12). The clergy are important, not because they are wiser or better or even more spiritual than other Christians. They are important because their ministry is to elicit, to encourage, and to direct the gifts of others in the servant ministry of the church.

Fourth, some of the erosion could be stopped, for Baptists at least, by revisiting and reaffirming the Baptist heritage. To hear again the voices of Smyth and Helwys, Spurgeon and Clifford, Backus and Leland, Carroll and Broadus, and Mullins and Truett could cause a rebirth of commitment to the doctrine of the priesthood of believers. If Baptists, like other groups before them, lose the idea of the priesthood of believers, it will not be because their heritage failed to include it. Their reactions to ecclesiastical authority, to infant baptism, to theological creedalism, and to state churches were motivated by a desire to protect the priesthood of believers.

If the Bible and Christian history tell us anything about our priesthood, they tell us that we should not take it for granted. Each generation of Christians must reassert and reclaim its priesthood. Some may want to strip you of your priesthood. The greater danger, however, is that you will quietly surrender it.

The Distortion of the Priesthood of Believers

Your role as priest is under threat of extinction not only by the forces of history. In our kind of world your priesthood is also subject to distortion by the way people think. Both the advocates and the critics of the doctrine of the priesthood of believers have at times distorted this biblical teaching. Luther had as much problem with some of those who followed him as with some of the Roman Catholics who opposed him.

A Christian doctrine is distorted when one aspect of it is emphasized while another aspect of it is ignored. Much harm has been done to Christian doctrines by individuals who get a complete grasp on a half-truth. The priesthood of believers is a two-handed doctrine, and distortion results from a one-handed approach.

Freedom and responsibility. Running throughout the doctrine of the priesthood of believers is the dual emphasis on freedom and responsibility. Like a coin, this doctrine has two sides. On one side of the coin of your priesthood is awesome freedom. On the other side is staggering responsibility.

You have the freedom to approach God through Jesus Christ for yourself. No one can force that decision on you. No one can keep you from that decision. Because of what Christ did, you can "with confidence draw near to the throne of grace" (Heb. 4:16). Through Jesus Christ, the apostle Paul said, everybody, Jew and Gentile alike, now has freedom of "access in one Spirit to the Father" (Eph. 2:18). Your freedom to be a priest is made possible by God's act on your behalf.

If, however, all you emphasize in the doctrine of the priesthood of believers is your freedom to choose Christ, you distort the doctrine. Priesthood also carries with it the immense responsibility to live under the lordship of Christ; to be holy, to "declare the wonderful deeds of him who called you out of darkness" (1 Pet. 2:9), and to take upon yourself the servant-life of Christ (Phil. 2:5-7).

This freedom-responsibility motif dominates every aspect of the priesthood of believers. In church life you have the freedom of equal privilege with other church members, but you also have the responsibility to exercise that freedom. In biblical interpretation you have the freedom of private interpretation, but you have the responsibility to study in order to

132

interpret the Bible correctly. In citizenship you have the freedom of religious expression, but you have the responsibility of civic participation.

Some distort the priesthood of believers by emphasizing freedom at the expense of responsibility. It is also possible, however, to distort the doctrine by stressing responsibility at the expense of freedom.

Individual and community. Very closely related to the freedom-responsibility theme in the priesthood of believers is the dual emphasis on individual and community. This dual emphasis is fundamental to a proper understanding of your priesthood. As far as the individual and the community are concerned, the priesthood of believers is a both-and doctrine. The individual cannot be denied; the community cannot be ignored. Our doctrine affirms individuals *in* community. The concept is distorted if one is emphasized at the expense of the other. A proper understanding of the priesthood of believers steers a middle course between the individualism that leads to arrogance and the authoritarianism of community that leads to puppetry.

Surely distortion occurs when the individual is taken out of community. To take the Christian out of the church is to take the priest out of the priesthood. The priesthood of believers, rightly understood, has never meant that Christianity is a home correspondence course in self-improvement. Religious individualism is not what this doctrine is about.

John Clifford, who I believe was one of the greatest Baptists who ever lived, is correct in referring positively to this doctrine as "sanctified individualism." With the Baptist vision of the Christian faith breathing on every word he spoke, Clifford said, "Freedom is inherent in the very conception of the spiritual life, and therefore there must be 'ample room and verge enough' within the territories of the Church for the full expression of an eager, intense, and sanctified individualism."[4] The Bible is clear that the Christian faith begins within the individual heart. So the story told as a joke and quoted by Marney has truth to it. ."The rabbi begins, 'Thus saith the *Lord!*' The priest begins, 'As the *Church* has always said. . . .' The average Protestant begins, 'Now, brethren, it seems to *me*. . . .'"[5] All three make an important point, but the

133

"sanctified individualism" reflected in the Protestant position is basic to your priesthood. What the Lord says through the church must be personalized in you!

Alongside the emphasis that every believer is a priest with individual access to God and His Word goes the corresponding truth that we are priests for one another and with one another. There is a horizontal as well as a vertical dimension to your priesthood. You are a part of what the Old Testament calls a "kingdom of priests" (Ex. 19:6) and what the New Testament calls a "royal priesthood" (1 Pet. 2:9). Individual priests are members of a corporate priesthood, which is the church. For individual priests to become wrapped up in the freedom of their personal relationships to God and forget their responsibility to and with the priesthood to minister in Christ's name is to distort what it means to be a priesthood of believers.

Laity and clergy. Another distortion of the priesthood of believers is that it is an anticlerical doctrine. But this doctrine does not set the laity over against the clergy. It is no effort to minimize the need for and the role of what is commonly referred to as professional ministers. Rather, it is an effort, as I have repeatedly said, to clarify the role of both the laity and the clergy. And this clarification is needed for the sake of both and for the good of the church. The doctrine of the priesthood of believers becomes anticlerical only if the clergy are transformed into monopolistic managers of the church, authoritative interpreters of Scripture, and sole mediators between God and human souls.

We are all priests. But we are not all the same kind of priests. The early Quakers of the seventeenth century radicalized the priesthood of believers and abolished the clergy altogether. That approach, of course, was a misunderstanding of the teachings of the Protestant Reformation. Both Luther and Calvin included the clergy *within* the universal priesthood. More importantly, the New Testament, especially the apostle Paul, stresses that the pastoral gift is one among the many gifts God bestows on His church to fulfill His mission (see Eph. 4:11-13). If we are not careful in explaining the meaning of the priesthood of believers for the ministry of the church, we will unwisely move toward the early Quaker mistake. On a popular level of stressing the universality of ministry we may unintentionally denigrate God's calling to the clergy, their need for theological education, and their need for financial support.

In truth, however, the greatest danger confronting Southern Baptists is not that of abolishing or even minimizing the role of the clergy. The greatest danger is that of minimizing the laity, ignoring the universality of the priesthood, and overlooking the New Testament teachings on spiritual gifts. There is something profoundly biblical about a church that prints the following in its bulletin:

Ministers: All the members of the church
Pastor: John Smith

The doctrine of the priesthood of believers does not exclude the clergy. It includes the laity.

Divine sovereignty and human activity. Occasionally, critics of the priesthood of believers distort the doctrine by saying that it elevates the human and ignores the divine. They say that it is a human-centered belief. Nothing misses the mark like this criticism. Much of this criticism is due to the phrase *soul competency* which is often used, especially in Baptist circles, as a synonym for the priesthood of believers. But as indicated in chapter 1, soul competency was never meant to convey an "I am the master of my fate; I am the captain of my soul" kind of philosophy. Rather, the very opposite is the case. Soul competency suggests that the individual soul is ultimately subject only to a sovereign God. Soul competency should always be interpreted as a competency under God.

Undergirding the entire concept of the priesthood of believers is the idea of divine initiative and divine calling. Returning to our pivotal Old Testament passage of Scripture, we see this clearly. In Exodus 19 God prefaces His announcement that Israel is to be a "kingdom of priests" with these words: " 'You have seen what I did to the Egyptians, and how I bore you on eagles' wings and brought you to myself' " (Ex. 19:4). And in the oft-referred-to priesthood passage of 1 Peter 2:9 the church is told, "You are a chosen race, a royal priesthood."

I remind you also that the five priesthood passages from the New Testament that we discussed in chapter 2 focus on Christ. The emphasis there is that we have become a priesthood by virtue of what Christ has done. God acted in Christ to create the priesthood. We act as a priesthood in response to what God has done and from the freedom and calling we have received. Again, that is why Martin Luther grounded his doctrine of the universal priesthood in justification by faith. And that is also why Baptists have based their understanding of the doctrine on the sovereignty of God.

Your freedom to approach God through Christ, your freedom to voice your convictions in the church, your freedom to exercise your spiritual gifts, and your freedom of conscience before the state—all these derive from God's gracious acts on your behalf. In the doctrine of the priesthood of believers divine sovereignty and human activity are joined.

The Implementation of the Priesthood of Believers

Spontaneity is an admirable characteristic of many black worship services. One feature of that spontaneity is the way the congregation encourages the preacher with verbal affirmations. It is not uncommon, when the black preacher reaches the point of applying the biblical or theological truth to the life situation of the people, to hear a member of the congregation shout, "Bring it home, Reverend, bring it home!"

I have made a determined effort throughout this book to bring home the scriptural doctrine of the priesthood of believers, to apply it to the life situation of Christians in general and of Southern Baptists in particular. It is not enough simply to know the biblical, theological, and historical foundations of this priceless doctrine. True, one of the reasons the doctrine does not get any more attention than it does is because many of us have been unaware of its place in the Bible, in Christian theology and history, and in the Baptist heritage. But we cannot end our study with only knowledge about the doctrine.

Our need corresponds to the bumper sticker on a clunker of an automobile I heard about. It said, "If you love Jesus, *push!* Honking is not enough!" Tipping our hats to the priesthood of believers is inadequate. We need to implement the doctrine, to integrate it into our personal discipleship, our corporate church and denominational life, and our citizenship in the nation. Let's summarize ways to do this.

Accessibility. To implement the priesthood of believers demands that we preach the biblical message that every individual has the right of personal, direct, and uncoerced access to God through Jesus Christ (1 Tim. 2:5). Race and sex and social status are not conditions of access (Gal. 3:28). No human priest can keep you from God, force you to God, or become a proxy for you before God. No substitutes are allowed. Accessibility to God is made possible by divine grace and is yours to choose. The priesthood begins with a marvelous mercy that is universally inclusive and intensely personal.

Equality. Accessibility leads to equality. To implement the priesthood of believers demands that we practice equality in the church. In Jesus Christ God not only acted to bring individual priests to Himself, but He also brought the priests to one another in a new kind of priesthood. Every priest stands on level ground under the one High Priest, Jesus Christ.

Every priest has an equal voice in the church, the right to express the mind of Christ as he or she understands it. No single priest, lay or clergy, has a monopoly on God's will for the priesthood. Individual priests may not have their way, but individual priests must have their say.

This issue of a priest having one's say relates to church government, but it also speaks to the right of private judgment in biblical interpretation. This right is not a license to believe anything, everything, or nothing; but it most assuredly is a shield from theological tyranny and authoritarianism.

To implement the priesthood of believers would also transform our worship expectations. Christian worship is not something the priesthood watches or hears. Christian worship is something the priesthood does.

Responsibility. Our priesthood takes the shape of a cross. Our word *accessibility,* as it relates to the priesthood of believers, represents the individual before God. The word *equality* refers to the priests in community with one another. But *responsibility* highlights the task the priesthood has to share the pain of the world in the redemptive spirit of Christ.

We priests of God were once exhorted by a prisoner-priest to "lead a life worthy of the calling" to which we have been called (Eph. 4:1). And the calling? I broke it down in chapter 5 into four different functions. But basically the calling is one: "'You shall love the Lord your God with all your heart, and with all your soul, and with all your strength, and with all your mind; and your neighbor as yourself'" (Luke 10:27).

Our pattern for our priestly calling is the one High Priest, Christ. He has sent us as He was sent: "'to preach good news to the poor . . . to proclaim release to the captives and recovering of sight to the blind, to set at liberty those who are oppressed, to proclaim the acceptable year of the Lord'" (Luke 4:18-19). The temple building of the old priesthood of Judaism has become a temple people (Eph. 2:21). We are that people, and our place of offering sacrifice is no longer at the altar of animal sacrifice. The place of sacrifice is now the world, and the sacrifices are our very lives (Rom. 12:1).

Universality. To implement the priesthood of believers is to be forced to redefine *minister* and *priests*. No longer is the priest the one who offers the sacrifices, administers the sacrament, or preaches the sermon. No longer is priesthood restricted to males from the tribe of Levi. The unmistakable teaching of the New Testament is that the old class-priesthood of Judaism has been transformed into the universal priesthood of all Christians.

The new priesthood—our priesthood—is no longer based on heredity or ordination or office, but on personal relationship to Jesus Christ and on the gifts that He distributes to all His people. To implement the priesthood of believers is to apply the priestly calling to *every* believer. It would mean that we would be rid of the deep cleavage between the clergy and the laity, because all are included in the priesthood, but with different functions. It would mean that we would stop loading up the clergy with all the work of the priesthood. And it would mean that we would encourage every believer to fill the role God wants that person to have in the priesthood.

To implement the conviction that every Christian in the body of Christ is called and gifted as a member of the priesthood would mean also that every local church would take more seriously the task of identifying and developing the gifts of the priesthood. Moreover, it would mean that individual priests would take advantage of the opportunities provided for sharpening their gifts.

Southern Baptists have a number of valuable resources for skill development and growth in discipleship. The ongoing periodicals for Adult Church Training are *Baptist Adults* and *Baptist Young Adults.* These Church Training resources provide a balanced diet of discipleship-training materials. By participating in adult groups, church members can grow in their understanding and can sharpen their skills. Priests of the Lord Jesus Christ need this kind of continuing training.

The Equipping Center system also offers many helpful resources for adult priests. This system is made up of many courses of study called Equipping Center modules. These modules are designed for short-term study by adults. Each study requires from four to thirteen weeks to complete. Equipping Center modules are available in the areas of Christian growth, family life, church and community, Christian doctrine, leadership, and evangelism and missions. These modules are designed to promote effective and interesting training for adult disciples. Training of this kind is important if adult Christians are to grow in their priesthood.

Believers who are ready for studies that require more time and discipline will find that MasterLife, MasterBuilder, and the LIFE system can help adult disciples continue to grow and develop their skills.

Most Southern Baptist churches provide opportunities for their people to learn and minister. In particular, the Brotherhood Commission and the Woman's Missionary Union provide channels for adult priesthood. These organizations focus on missions and ministry. The Brotherhood Commission helps men and boys to get involved in vital ministries of the church. The Woman's Missionary Union provides education in missions and practical mission-action opportunities in the community for women and girls.

The priesthood of believers also is expressed in financial and prayer support of foreign and home missions. Many churches now send teams and individuals to do missions work in a direct way. Information about direct missions involvement by church members can be obtained from the Foreign Mission Board and the Home Mission Board.

Liberty. Finally, to implement the doctrine of the priesthood

139

of believers would clarify the Christian's relationship to the nation. No nation in the world, including our own, is the chosen people of God. The church of Jesus Christ, with its worldwide discipleship, is the elect nation. The universal priesthood of Christ is without political distinction or national boundaries. Christ and Caesar must never be equated.

From Caesar the priesthood asks liberty of conscience for itself and for all people. To Caesar the priesthood promises responsible citizenship. Before Caesar the priesthood affirms only one sovereignty, the Lord Jesus Christ.

We should not be discouraged if the priesthood of believers is difficult to implement. I remind you that the New Testament passages in which this doctrine appears most often are located in what we have called the literature of persecution—Hebrews, 1 Peter, and Revelation. Early Christians turned to this doctrine when they were in times of stress and struggle. Martin Luther rediscovered this doctrine in turbulent times, and seventeenth-century Baptists reaffirmed this doctrine in the trauma of their own birth pains.

The conditions of our culture—traumatic or tranquil, good or bad—do not alter our calling. We are "priests of God and of Christ" (Rev. 20:6), "a holy priesthood" (1 Pet. 2:5), "a royal priesthood" (1 Pet. 2:9). Is there a greater privilege? Or a greater responsibility? Little wonder that the last book in the Bible begins with such praise: "To him who loves us and has freed us from our sins by his blood and made us a kingdom, priests to his God and Father, to him be glory and dominion for ever and ever. Amen" (Rev. 1:5-6).

PERSONAL LEARNING ACTIVITY 14

Review pages 136-140. In this section of the book the author uses several words to describe the effect that implementing the doctrine of the priesthood of believers would have in the life of a Christian today. Beside each word, write a definition that relates to the doctrine of the priesthood of believers.

Accessibility _____

_____

Equality _____

_____

Responsibility _____

_____

Universality _____

_____

Liberty _____

_____

Notes

1. Nelvin Vos, *Seven Days a Week: Faith in Action* (Philadelphia: Fortress Press, 1985), 27.

2. *The Holy Bible,* Revised Standard Version (Nashville: Holman Bible Publishers, 1982).

3. Robert E. Slocum, *Ordinary Christians in a High-Tech World* (Waco, Texas: Word Books, 1986), 42.

4. John Clifford, "The Baptist World Alliance: Its Origin and Character, Meaning and Work," *The Life of Baptists in the Life of the World,* ed. Walter B. Shurden (Nashville: Broadman Press, 1985), 38.

5. Carlyle Marney, *Priests to Each Other* (Valley Forge: The Judson Press, 1974), 42. Used by permission of Judson Press.

Teaching Guide

Arthur H. Criscoe

Introduction

This teaching guide contains detailed teaching plans to assist you in leading a group study of *The Doctrine of the Priesthood of Believers*. The plans can be used with either a large or a small group.

The teaching plans in this guide are self-contained—that is, they enable you to lead good sessions without additional resources. However, *The Doctrine of the Priesthood of Believers—Teaching Workbook* is highly recommended. The teaching workbook contains a supply of overhead cel masters, worksheet masters, teaching posters, and discussion cards. These resources provide visual aids to enrich the sessions and other tools to involve group members actively in the learning process. Group size is no problem; the resources are effective with large auditorium groups and with small groups in a classroom. Only one copy of the teaching workbook is needed. The cel masters, worksheet masters, posters, and discussion cards may be reproduced. Suggestions for using all of the resources are included in the teaching workbook.

Learning Goals

Upon completion of this course, each group member should have a better understanding of the doctrine of the priesthood of believers and its implications for his or her life and also should become personally involved in implementing the doctrine.

Each session has a specific learning goal related to this general goal. The learning goals will help you to maintain a focus as you lead the sessions. They also afford a means by which participants can measure their progress along the way.

Planning Actions

1. Nothing can substitute for study and prayer. Pray for the guidance of the Holy Spirit as you prepare for and lead the sessions.

   In addition to this book by Walter B. Shurden and *The Doctrine of the Priesthood of Believers—Teaching Workbook,* two Broadman cassette tapes are available: "The Doctrine of the Priesthood of Believers." These cassette tapes by William H. Stephens are designed to give you, the leader, background and supplementary information on the doctrine.

2. Encourage the participants to read the appropriate chapters in *The Doctrine of the Priesthood of Believers* in preparation for each session.

3. Prepare a poster outline of the session titles to use in all of the sessions. Prepare a 1 by 4 arrow pointer from poster board and glue the arrow to a clothespin. Use this pointer with the outline poster.

THE PRIESTHOOD OF BELIEVERS

Session 1: An Autobiography
      (Chapter 1)
Session 2: The Bible and Salvation
      (Chapters 2 and 3)
Session 3: The Church
      (Chapter 4)
Session 4: The Christian Life and Spiritual Gifts
      (Chapters 5-6)
Session 5: The State and Your World
      (Chapter 7-8)

---

4. The ideas for the teaching posters in each session of this guide are taken from *The Doctrine of the Priesthood of Believers—Teaching Workbook.* Only one set, of posters is needed for the study.

5. If you have a large number of persons in the study, small-group work can be handled easily. Simply divide into as many small groups as necessary to get everyone involved.

The same assignment can be given to more than one small group. For example, if the teaching plan calls for five small groups to be given five assignments and you have one hundred persons in the study, go ahead and form twenty-five small groups. Five groups would be given the first assignment, five groups the second assignment, and so on.

6. Make extensive use of the Bible as you teach. It is our textbook for studying the doctrine of the priesthood of believers. The Bible alone is our authority for faith and practice.

7. Begin and close each session with prayer.

8. Following each session, spend some time evaluating the session. Think of ways you can improve future sessions.

Session 1
An Autobiography
Chapter 1

Learning goal: After completing this session, participants should understand the doctrine of the priesthood of believers. They will be able to: (1) define and describe the doctrine of the priesthood of believers; (2) explain in their own words the origin of the doctrine of the priesthood of believers in biblical teachings; and (3) describe in their own words the development of the doctrine of the priesthood of believers in Christian history in general and by Baptists in particular.

Before the Session

1. Have copies of *The Doctrine of the Priesthood of Believers* available for participants. Have registration materials and a Baptist Doctrine Diploma available.
2. Prepare a copy of the following true/false pretest for each member (or use worksheet 1 in *Teaching Workbook*). (1) Every Christian is to relate to God, but not all Christians are to act for God. (2) The doctrine of the priesthood of believers came into existence during the Protestant Reformation. (3) The title of *priest* is used by New Testament writers to refer to a select and special group of Christians. (4) Every Christian is a priest. (5) The calling of the priesthood of believers is to worship and to witness. (6) Every person has the privilege of uncoerced personal access to God's grace. (7) Salvation is personal in nature. (8) No person can be forced to believe. (9) Mission to the world has always been at the center of God's call to His people. (10) All believers have a right to equal privileges in the church. (11) All members do not have an equal voice in the church. (12) All Christians are responsible for ministry. (13) Confrontation has no place in Christian ministry. (14) Spiritual gifts are assigned to Christians by the church. (15) Every Christian has one or more spiritual gifts. (16) Both the state and God constitute loyalties for the Christian. (17) Authentic faith cannot be coerced or denied by the state. (18) The state is

the source of liberty. (19) The doctrine of the priesthood of believers emphasizes both freedom and responsibility. (20) There is a horizontal dimension to the world as well as a vertical dimension to God in our priesthood.

3. Prepare the following agree/disagree statements (or use worksheet 2 in *Teaching Workbook*). You can write the statements on the chalkboard; you can write them on adding-machine tape; or you can make copies to hand out. (1) The words *priest* and *priesthood* are not Baptist words. (2) Not all Christians have the right of direct and immediate access to God through Christ. (3) The priesthood of believers demands responsible participation in church life. (4) The priesthood of believers has no relationship to the priesthood of Israel in the Old Testament. (5) God ordained that only men from the tribe of Levi would be priests in Old Testament times. (6) The word *priest* is used in the New Testament to refer to clergy. (7) Early in Christian history the church began to stress the priesthood of *some* believers rather than the priesthood of *all* believers. (8) Only Baptists have emphasized the doctrine of the priesthood of believers.

4. Write the following statements on large sheets of newsprint. (1) The priesthood of believers is the centerpiece of the Baptist faith. (2) A priest is someone who relates to and acts for God. (3) All believers are priests. (4) Spectator religion is out. (5) Each Christian has a duty to hand on the gospel. (6) "The veil of the temple was rent in the midst" (Luke 23:45).* Do not number the statements. Mount these teaching posters in random order on the walls around the room.

During the Session

1. Quickly care for administrative matters. Distribute copies of *The Doctrine of the Priesthood of Believers*. Show the Baptist Doctrine Diploma and explain how the diploma is earned and encourage everyone to earn one.

2. Use the outline poster to overview the entire study. Share the general learning goal for the entire study. Focus on session 1.

3. Ask volunteers to read the agree/disagree statements aloud. As each statement is read, determine those who

agree with the statement, those who disagree, and those who are undecided. If the group is divided in opinion, allow time for discussion of the statement.

4. Define *priest, priesthood, believers,* and *the priesthood of believers,* using the definitions in chapter 1. Ask members to find as many answers as they can to the question "Who Am I?" in chapter 1 (for example, "I am your right to choose Christ for yourself"). Write the answers on the chalkboard as they are called out. Allow time for discussion.

5. Summarize briefly the section "Where Did I Come From?" Allow time for discussion.

6. Call attention to the teaching posters on the walls. Ask volunteers to read the statements and to comment on their meanings.

7. Distribute the pretest and ask members to complete it before the next session. (Answers are in ses. 5.)

----

*KJV

Session 2
The Bible and Salvation
Chapters 2 and 3

Learning goal: After completing this session, participants should understand the biblical teachings on the priesthood of believers and the significance of this doctrine for salvation. They will be able to: (1) summarize in their own words the Old and New Testament teachings on priesthood; (2) describe the priesthood of Christ; and (3) explain the significance of the priesthood of believers for salvation.

Before the Session

1. Prepare the following agree/disagree statements (or use worksheet 3 in *Teaching Workbook*). (1) The Old Testament priesthood symbolized the worthiness of the nation Israel. (2) Old Testament priests were mediators, not interpreters. (3) The priesthood of believers is hierarchical, not hereditary. (4) Our priesthood is rooted in Christ. (5) Jesus is priest by virtue of Levite origins. (6) The phrase *the priesthood of believers* is not found in the Bible. (7) Equality of access to God's grace for salvation is not rooted in human capability. (8) To emphasize individualism is to deny community. (9) There is no such thing as forced love. (10) A person cannot accept salvation without accepting priesthood.

2. Prepare the following teaching posters. Mount them in random order on the walls. (1) Old Testament priests were mediators who brought the people to God. (2) Old Testament priests were teachers who brought God to the people. (3) Jesus is our Great High Priest. (4) Good priesting is impossible without identification. (5) Not even death overcame the priestly work of Christ. (6) Priesthood comes with pardon. (7) Accessibility to God leads to equality among believers. (8) We are saved one by one, person by person. (9) You can't send another priest to bring God's grace to you. (10) The freedom to choose to believe is at the heart of the Bible. (11) God leaves the front gate open. (12) "Whosoever will may come."

149

During the Session

1. Call attention to the outline poster. Focus on session 2. Use the agree/disagree statements as a basis for discussion.

2. Ask one third of the group to work in pairs to discover under the topic "The theological roots of priesthood" three things the Jewish priesthood symbolized. Ask another one third of the group to work in pairs to discover the two primary functions of the priesthood. Ask the remaining one third of the group to work in pairs to discover the structure of the priesthood. Allow time for group work and call for reports.

3. Summarize the high priesthood of Christ, using the three-point outline in the book.

4. Divide members into five small groups. Assign each group one of the following passages: 1 Peter 2:5; 1 Peter 2:9; Revelation 1:5-6; Revelation 5:9-10; Revelation 20:6. Ask each group to study its verse(s) for the identification, character, and vocation of the priesthood. Allow time for group work and call for reports.

5. Lecture briefly on the significance of the priesthood of believers for salvation, using the three-point outline in chapter 3.

6. Refer to personal learning activity (PLA) 4. Allow a brief time for participants to complete this activity. Lead in a discussion of this activity.

7. Ask volunteers to read the teaching posters and to comment on their meanings.

Session 3
The Church
Chapter 4

Learning goal: After completing this session, participants should understand the significance of the priesthood of believers for the church. They will be able to: (1) state to whom the church belongs and (2) explain the significance of the priesthood of believers for church government, the Bible, the church ordinances, and worship.

Before the Session

1. Prepare the following agree/disagree statements (or use worksheet 4 in *Teaching Workbook*). (1) Your business with God is not simply *your* business. (2) Television preachers and the "electronic church" undercut the role of community in church life. (3) Most radio and TV ministries strengthen the local church. (4) The church is an institution, not a building. (5) We are called to be God's people in a communal setting. (6) The mission and purpose of the church relate to the world. (7) The local church is the only meaning of *church* in the New Testament. (8) There is no church apart from mission. (9) Baptists are an anticreedal people. (10) Only an ordained pastor or evangelist should administer baptism.

2. Prepare the following teaching posters. Mount them in random order on the walls. (1) The priesthood of believers is not spiritual lone rangerism. (2) The church is the church of the living God. (3) The church is the people, on Monday as well as on Sunday. (4) We are called to be God's people in a communal setting. (5) There were footprints on the beach before we walked on shore. (6) There is no hierarchy in the priesthood.

During the Session

1. Call attention to the outline poster. Focus on session 3. Use the agree/disagree statements as a basis for discussion.
2. Summarize the topic "Whose Church Is This?"
3. Refer to PLA 6. Allow a brief time for participants to

complete it. Lead the group to discuss the activity.

4. Divide members into four small groups. Ask each group to discover the significance of the priesthood of believers for one of the following: church government, the Bible, the church ordinances, and worship. Allow time for group work and call for reports. Use PLA 7 as part of the discussion. Also spend a few minutes analyzing the worship services of your church in light of the study.

5. Ask volunteers to read the teaching posters and to comment on their meanings.

Session 4
The Christian Life and Spiritual Gifts
Chapters 5 and 6

Learning goal: After completing this session, participants should understand the significance of the priesthood of believers for the Christian life and for spiritual gifts. They will be able to: (1) explain the priesthood as servants, heralds, confessors, and prophets; (2) summarize the biblical teachings on spiritual gifts, including their universality, diversity, purpose, and development; and (3) explain the role of the pastor and other vocational Christian workers in the church.

Before the Session

1. Prepare the following agree/disagree statements (or use worksheet 5 in *Teaching Workbook*). (1) Our priesthood is incomplete unless we speak of our faith in Christ. (2) Serving is more important than speaking. (3) Only someone with proper training should serve as a confessor. (4) Confrontation has no place in priesthood. (5) The ministry of redemptive criticism is not biblical. (6) The biggest enemy of the contemporary church is staleness, not unbelief. (7) Every Christian, including children, has received at least one spiritual gift. (8) Every Christian is charismatic. (9) There are no spiritual gifts other than those named in the Bible. (10) The pastor is to equip others for ministry.

2. Prepare the following teaching posters. Mount them in random order on the walls. (1) Faith is no private possession to hoard. (2) We are not catch basins but conduits. (3) We are ambassadors for Christ. (4) Priesthood involves prophethood. (5) We priests are hosts, not guests. (6) Priesthood is freighted with responsibility. (7) Each child of God is gifted. (8) Gifts come from God. (9) Christian discipleship is not a spectator's sport. (10) Gifts come in different shapes, forms, and styles. (11) Conformity in the body is actually deformity. (12) What God puts in your hands is to be used in

life. (13) God's gifts are not to be buried in the ground.

3. If you are the pastor, prepare a brief testimony of your work as an equipper. Include the following: (1) your biggest thrill as an equipper; (2) your biggest disappointment as an equipper; (3) how others have received your equipping ministry; and (4) what can be done to develop more fully your equipping ministry. If you are not the pastor, enlist him to be present and share a brief testimony based on the points above.

During the Session

1. Call attention to the outline poster. Focus on session 4. Use the agree/disagree statements as a basis for discussion.

2. Divide members into four small groups. Assign each group one aspect or role of our priesthood: servants, heralds, confessors, prophets. Ask each group to study its assigned role and to be prepared to answer the following questions: (1) Exactly what is the nature of this aspect or role? (2) How did Jesus serve in this role? (3) What are some things that make it easy for us to serve in this role? (4) What are some things that make it difficult to serve in this role?

3. Move into the study of chapter 6 by leaving members in the four small groups. Assign each group one scriptural concept related to spiritual gifts: universality, diversity, purpose, and development. Ask members to find scriptural support for each concept.

4. If you are the pastor, share the brief testimony you prepared. If you have your pastor with you, ask him to share his testimony, based on the points you gave him.

5. Ask volunteers to read the teaching posters and to comment on their meanings.

Session 5
The State and Your World
Chapters 7 and 8

Learning goal: After completing this session, participants should understand the significance of the priesthood of believers for the Christian in relationship to the state and how to implement the doctrine of the priesthood of believers in today's world. They will be able to: (1) identify three theological foundations for religious liberty; (2) describe four patterns of church-state relations; (3) explain the Christian's responsibility to the state; (4) describe how the priesthood of believers can become distorted; and (5) name five key actions a Christian can take to implement the priesthood of believers.

Before the Session

1. Prepare the following agree/disagree statements (or use worksheet 6 in *Teaching Workbook*). (1) A Christian does not owe allegiance to the state. (2) Loyalty to the state and loyalty to the lordship of Christ are compatible. (3) Christianity in the first century was a subversive, rather than a supportive, element in the Roman Empire. (4) The acceptance of Christ as Lord makes all human institutions less than absolute. (5) Our freedom in Christ does not exempt us from the laws of the state. (6) A Christian should always obey the laws of the state. (7) Christianity is dependent for its survival on a democratic form of government. (8) Religious freedom for Baptists is based on the idea of human reason and the need for a society of equals. (9) The state is the source of liberty. (10) No person can give another human being liberty. (11) The right not to believe is as sacred as one's right to believe. (12) The best pattern of church-state relations is that of the church above the state. (13) Government should not reflect the religious sentiments of its citizenry. (14) The distinctions between church and state are blurred by Christians who hold public office. (15) The separation of church and state should not be interpreted as the disengagement of Christians from the affairs of

government. (16) The priesthood of believers can become distorted by an emphasis on freedom alone. (17) The doctrine of the priesthood of believers emphasizes the individual, not the community. (18) Soul competency refers to human achievement and capability.

2. Prepare the following teaching posters. Mount them in random order on the walls. (1) A free church in a free state is the Christian ideal. (2) God alone is Lord of the conscience. (3) Christ, not Caesar, is Lord. (4) "The King is a mortall man, and not God."* (5) Discipleship does not negate citizenship. (6) The temple has always been downtown. (7) No one else can do your discipleship for you. (8) There is a horizontal as well as a vertical dimension to your priesthood. (9) Every priest stands on level ground. (10) Our priesthood takes the shape of the cross. (11) Christ and Caesar must never be equated.

3. Prepare a lecture on "Liberty from the State."
Use the following outline.
   a. Foundations for religious liberty
      (1) Nature of God
      (2) Nature of persons
      (3) Nature of faith
   b. Areas of religious freedom
      (1) Freedom *of* religion
      (2) Freedom *from* religion
      (3) Freedom *for* religion
   c. Patterns of church-state relations
      (1) Church above state
      (2) Church under state
      (3) Alliance of church with state
      (4) Church and state side by side

4. Reproduce the pretest used in session 1 for use in this session as a posttest.

During the Session

1. Call attention to the outline poster. Review the study and focus on session 5. Use the agree/disagree statements as a basis for discussion.
2. Lecture briefly on "Liberty from the State." Allow time for discussion.

3. Point out from chapter 8 four ways the priesthood of believers can become distorted. Draw a chart on the chalkboard with *Freedom* over one column and *Responsibility* over another column (or use worksheet 7 in *Teaching Workbook*). Involve participants in discussing these two concerns as they relate to church life, biblical interpretation, and citizenship. Summarize responses on the chart.

4. Ask volunteers to read the teaching posters and to comment on their meanings.

5. Allow a brief time for those who have not done so to complete PLA 14. Review and summarize the entire study by discussing this activity. Hand out the posttest and allow time for members to complete it. Discuss the answers. Answers: 1. F, 2. F, 3. F, 4. T, 5. T, 6. T, 7. T, 8. T, 9. T, 10. T, 11. F, 12. T, 13. F, 14. F, 15. T, 16. T, 17. T, 18. F, 19. T, 20. T.

6. Express appreciation to members for their participation in the study.

---

*Sydnor L. Stealey, ed. and comp., *A Baptist Treasury* (New York: Thomas Y. Crowell Company, 1958), 12-13.

The Church Study Course

The Church Study Course is a Southern Baptist educational system consisting of short courses for adults and youth combined with a credit and recognition system. More than five hundred courses are available in twenty-three subject areas. Credit is awarded for each course completed. These credits may be applied to one or more of over one hundred diploma plans in the recognition system. Diplomas are available for most leadership positions, and general diplomas are available for all Christians. These diplomas certify that a person has completed from five to eight prescribed courses.

Complete details about the Church Study Course system, courses available, and diplomas offered and diploma requirements may be found in a current copy of Church Study Course Catalog and in the study course section of Church Materials Catalog. Study course materials are available from Baptist Book Stores.

The Church Study Course system is sponsored by the Sunday School Board, the Woman's Missionary Union, and the Brotherhood Commission of the Southern Baptist Convention.

How to Request Credit for This Course

This book is the text for course 05059 in the subject area Baptist Doctrine. This course is designed for a minimum of five hours of group study.

Requirements for Credit

Credit may be earned in two ways.

1. *Group study.* Read the book and attend group sessions. If you are absent from one or more sessions, complete the learning activities for the material missed.

2. *Individual study.* Read the book and complete the learning activities. Written work should be submitted to an appropriate church leader.

To Request Credit

A request for credit may be made on Form 725, Church Study Course Enrollment/Credit Request, and sent to the Awards Office, Sunday School Board, 127 Ninth Avenue, North, Nashville, TN 37234. The form on the following page may be used to request credit.

A record of your awards will be maintained by the Awards Office. Four times each year copies will be sent to churches for distribution to members.

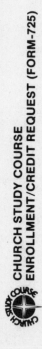

CHURCH STUDY COURSE
ENROLLMENT/CREDIT REQUEST (FORM-725)

PERSONAL CSC NUMBER (If Known)

INSTRUCTIONS:
1. Please PRINT or TYPE.
2. COURSE CREDIT REQUEST—Requirements must be met. Use exact title.
3. ENROLLMENT IN DIPLOMA PLANS—Enter selected diploma title to enroll.
4. For additional information see the Church Study Course Catalog.
5. Duplicate additional forms as needed. Free forms are available from the Awards Office and State Conventions.

TYPE OR REQUEST: (Check all that apply)
- ☐ Course Credit
- ☐ Enrollment in Diploma Plan
- ☐ Address Change
- ☐ Name Change
- ☐ Church Change

REQUEST FOR

- ☐ Mr. ☐ Miss.
- ☐ Mrs.

DATE OF BIRTH ➤

Month	Day	Year

Name (First, Mi, Last)

Street, Route, or P.O. Box

City, State, Zip Code

CHURCH

Church Name

Mailing Address

City, State, Zip Code

COURSE CREDIT REQUEST

Course No.	Use Exact title
05059	1 *The Doctrine of the Priesthood of Believers*
Course No.	Use Exact title
	2.
Course No.	Use Exact title
	3.
Course No.	Use Exact title
	4.
Course No.	Use Exact title
	5.

ENROLLMENT IN DIPLOMA PLANS

If you have not previously indicated a diploma(s) you wish to earn, or you are beginning to work on a new one(s), select and enter the diploma title from the current Church Study Course Catalog. Select one that relates to your leadership responsibility or interest. When all requirements have been met, the diploma will be automatically mailed to your church. No charge will be made for enrollment or diplomas.

Title of diploma	Age group or area
1.	
Title of diploma	Age group or area
2.	
Signature of Pastor, Teacher, or study Leader	Date

MAIL THIS REQUEST TO ➤

CHURCH STUDY COURSE AWARDS OFFICE
RESEARCH SERVICES DEPARTMENT
127 NINTH AVENUE, NORTH
NASHVILLE, TENNESSEE 37234

FORM-725 (rev. 7-83)